Ulysses:

Episode 3, "Proteus":

The 1922 Text

Supplemental Notes & Commentary

Jack Grapes

Bombshelter Press

Los Angeles 2022

Second Edition

ISBN: 978-0-941017-44-2

Bombshelter Press
www.bombshelterpress.com
books@bombshelterpress.com
6684 Colgate Ave
Los Angeles, California 90048 USA
Printed in the United States of America

Cover painting of James Joyce in Zurich by Conrad Ruf, circa 1918, scan courtesy of the Division of Rare and Manuscript Collections at Cornell University.
Author photograph on back cover by Alexis Rhone Fancher.
Layout by Alan Berman.

Contents

Dublin's pedestrian-only Ha'Penny Bridge; beyond it, the dome of the 18th-century Custom House & Liberty Hall.

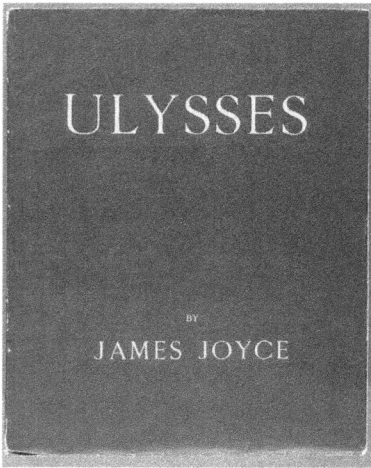

Sylvia Beach, owner of Shakespeare and Company, which first published the book, described the trouble this blue cover caused: "Joyce's natural desire to have his book dressed in the Greek blue was one of worst difficulties. Who would have dreamed that the lovely blue of the Greek flag was not to be found? Again and again Darantiere [the printer] came up to Paris and we matched blues, only to discover that the new sample didn't go with the Greek flag, which was kept flying at Shakespeare and Company in honor of Odysseus. Alas! merely to look at that flag gave me a headache. Darantiere's search took him to Germany, where it ended with the discovery of the right blue—but this time it was the wrong paper. He solved this problem by getting the color lithographed on white cardboard, which explains why the insides of the covers were white."

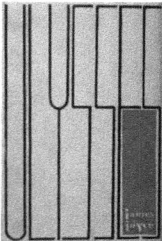

1934, designed by Ernst Reichl, Random House

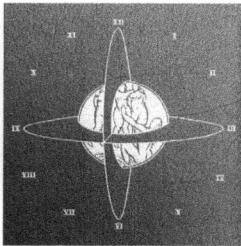

1935, designed by Henri Matisse, Limited Edition Club

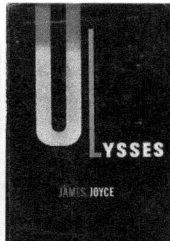

1946, designed by E McKnight Kauffer, Random House

1968, Penguin

1984, Penguin

1998, Oxford World Classics

2000, Penguin

2012, Alma Classics

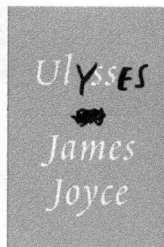

2013, designed by Peter Mendelsund, Vintage

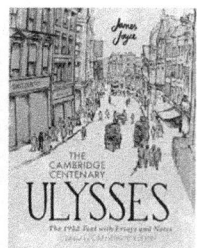

2022, Random House

Are You Going to Read *Ulysses?*
Yes I Said Yes I Will Yes

Controversial, scandalous, erudite and funny, *Ulysses* is indisputedly a landmark of twentieth-century modernism. It charts one day—16th June 1904—in the lives of three inhabitants of Dublin: the advertising salesman Leopold Bloom, the artist Stephen Dedalus, and the lusty Molly Bloom, Leopold Bloom's wife. Their peregrinations, thoughts, and encounters form the basis of the narrative, which becomes a celebration of all human experience through the lives of specific individuals in a specific place at a specific time. *Ulysses* is both an experimental novel and a book intimately concerned with the events of modern life. If you don't have a copy of *Ulysses* (Joyce pronounced it *ooo*lysses), now is the time to get one. Why? Because it's been voted the greatest novel of the 20th century, if not of all time. Should you read it? Yes. Why? Because it's the greatest novel of all time.

Is it difficult to read? Sometimes yes, sometimes no. At times it's funny, dramatic, lyrical, erudite, philosophical, scandalous, blasphemous, and downright obscene. But it also includes scenes you'll never forget: Buck Mulligan's mock-mass atop the Martello Tower; Stephen's imagined visit to his uncle's house; Leopold Bloom's erotic fantasies in the butcher shop; the funeral in Glasnevin Cemetery; Leopold masturbating in his pants while watching Gerty McDowell flash her undergarments; Molly's afternoon tryst with Blazes Boylan; Leopold and Stephen sharing a cup of Epps cocoa in the kitchen and peeing under the night sky in their garden; Molly's midnight soliloquy in bed as Leopold sleeps beside her, head to foot, feet to head. The humanity of those three characters stay with the reader despite all the linguistic wizardy and experimental literary effects.

Which edition should you get? Preferably the Random House Modern Library edition published in 1934 after Judge Woolsey had ruled that *Ulysses* was not obscene and cleared the book for distribution in the United States, concluding that "after long reflection, even though the effect of *Ulysses* on the reader is undoubtedly somewhat emetic, nowhere does it tend to be an aphrodisiac." The 1961 Modern Library edition was scrupulously corrected, the type reset and new plates were made. In 1992, it was reissued again. It's easy to handle, the print is readable, and the book is sturdy.

The Oxford World's Classics edition published in 1998 is a facsimile copy of the 1922 original text with detailed explanatory notes in the back, episode by episode. The paperback edition is close to a thousand pages, so it can be bulky in the hand, the text of the 1922 printing is somewhat small, but readable, and there's a good introduction by Jeri Johnson.

The Alma Classic edition published and revised in 2012 was based on the 1939 Odyssey Press Edition which used the text from the British first edition published by the Bodley Head in 1936. It too has explanatory notes in the back, chapter by chapter, provided by Sam Slote, Marc A. Mamigonian and John Turner. It is not a facsimile of that edition, so the pagination is different, but the original page numbers are indicated in the margins. They also use the newspaper headlines in "Aeolus" Episode 7 from the original Shakespeare and Co. 1922 first printing. But again, the whole book is over 800 pages, it's thick and bulky with a stiff spine, making it hard to handle when reading. That's why I go back to the Random House Modern Library version, though it has no explanatory notes. For explanatory notes, still the best is Don Gifford's *Ulysses Annotated*, published 1988.

Some prefer the Gabler Edition, published in 1986, which contains corrections to more than 5,000 errors in earlier editions. Almost as soon as *Ulysses* first appeared, in Paris in 1922, James Joyce began to compile a list of errata, and publishers have continued the process of correcting errors ever since, but in the process, inadvertently adding as many errors as were corrected. In 1974, an international team of scholars headed by Professor Hans Walter Gabler began to study manuscript evidence, typescripts, and proofs in order to produce as accurate and as complete a new edition as possible. The Gabler edition was hailed as a monumental achievement, one that made this great and complex novel more accessible and enjoyable than ever before. But controversy followed, and arguments for both the Random House Modern Library edition and the Gabler edition were contentious, hot-tempered, and at times, hostile. (See the essay following the notes.)

Due for publication in 2022 is the *The Cambridge Centenary Ulysses: The 1922 Text with Essays and Notes*. This new edition features a facsimile of the historic 1922 Shakespeare and Company text, including Joyce's own errata as well as references to amendments made in later editions. It will also come equipped with maps, photographs, and explanatory footnotes, providing a vivid and illuminating context for the experiences of Leopold Bloom, Stephen Dedalus, and Molly Bloom on that day in June 16, 1904.

Our focus in this workbook will be on Episode 3, which displays the technique of "stream of consciousness," pioneered by Dorothy Richardson in her sequence of 13 semi-autobiographical novels published between 1915 and 1967. Though she was one of the earliest modernist novelists to use stream of consciousness as a narrative technique, it was not fully realized until Joyce used it in *Ulysses*. Joyce himself credited Édouard Dujardin, one of the early users of the stream of consciousness literary technique, exemplified by his 1888 novel *Les Lauriers sont coupés* (translated in the English edition as *We Will to the Woods No More*).

The first two episodes of *Ulysses* are relatively straight-forward with patches of "interior monologue" and "stream of consciousness," but those narrative techniques are not used as extensively in the first two episodes as they appear in Episode 3, the use of which nearly overwhelms the casual reader. First-time readers of the book (Joyce never referred to it as a novel, he always called it "the book.") manage to get through episodes one and two without too much trouble, though in 1922 and for decades afterwards, the experimental and avant-garde style put off a lot of readers. Today, we're a little more used to writing that delves into interior monologue and even stream of consciousness. But Episode 3 is a deal breaker. That's when most readers give up. But don't give up. See it through. Read that episode not just for the story, but for the experience. Don't be afraid of having to let go of the expectation of the usual narrative experience. "Consciousness" is much more complex than narrative, linear "thoughts." Consciousness involves the discordant music of fragmented imagery, the disconnected associations of random ideas, myriad bodily sensations, as well as the thought process we speak to ourselves, one thought after another, what is called in narrative technique the more conventional "interior monologue." Consciousness is symphonic. Allow yourself to fall into its music. You will come back to Episode 3 again and again and each time you will get more out of it. After that, the rest of the novel—oooops, sorry, the "book"—will be so much easier. Reading *OOO-LYSSES* is an "experience."

In the first episode, we meet Stephen Dadalus, Joyce's alter-ego as a young man, ready to embark on his life as a writer. The novel takes place on one day, June 16, 1904, which is the day Joyce met Nora Barnacle, with whom he left for the Continent to pursue his life as an artist. As the book opens, Stephen has left home and is now staying for a few days with Buck Mulligan, his friend, who had rented a Martello Tower on the seacoast of Ireland.

As Mulligan explains to a roomate named Haines, also staying at the Tower, the "Martello" towers that line the Irish coast at intervals north and south of Dublin (12 to the north, 16 to the south) were built in the early years of the 19th century by the British government under the leadership of "Billy Pitt" (Prime Minister William Pitt the Younger), to protect against the threat of invasion "when the French were on the sea," referring back to the The Napoleonic Wars between Britain and France, which had been brewing ever since the French Revolution. Fearing that French forces would invade to assist the cause of Irish revolution, as they had in the 1790s, the British constructed a series of small defensive fortifications along the coasts of England and Ireland, beginning in 1803 and ending with Pitt's death in 1806. The tower at Sandycove, by some accounts, was the first built in Ireland, to protect the approaches to Dublin. If true, this primacy may partly explain Mulligan's saying that "ours is the *omphalos*" (i.e., the navel or source of all the others). The British took as their model for all these fortifications a squat round tower constructed by the Genovese at Punta Mortella (Myrtle Point) in Corsica, which two of their warships had tried to destroy in 1794. Their combined firepower of 104 guns failed to disable the tower. Most defensive fortifications enjoy the advantage of height: they can fire down on attacking ships, while the ships' guns must use a good portion of their power (and risk explosive rupture of the barrel) simply to overcome gravity. In addition, the design of this tower was brilliant. Its roundness, combined with a gentle slope inward from base to top, deflected much of the power of incoming shot, and whatever force was not deflected was absorbed by exceptionally thick walls. Additionally, its round artillery platform meant that it could direct fire around an unlimited arc. After two and a half hours of close bombardment, the HMS *Fortitude* was badly damaged by shot from the tower's two eighteen-pounders, and the warships were forced to withdraw. By Joyce's time, many of these towers could be leased and used as living quarters.

When Lori and I went to Ireland a few years ago for the Bloomsday celebration, we visited the Martello Tower south of Dublin, the one in which Joyce stayed for those few nights. It is now a James Joyce Museum. I climbed the narrow stone steps to the top, where the huge cannon would have been, which is where the first scene of *Ulysses* takes place, as Buck Mulligan takes his morning shave. In the novel, Stephen is upset because Haines had a nightmare causing him to discharge a pistol barely missing Stephen. His ultimatum: Either Haines goes or I go! The three take their breakfast and head down to the beach for a swim. Joyce gives Buck Mulligan the only key, implying that it was Stephen who would go, who was "usurped," who would now be homeless.

In Episode 2, Stephen walks a few miles to the boys school in Dalkey where he teaches. One of the peculiarities of *Ulysses* is the time spent by Joycean scholars concerning themselves with Joyce's philosophical and literary references—in Episode 3 alone Stephen's consciousness ping-pongs from the philosophy of Aristotle to the philosophical concepts propounded by Jacob Boehme, Hegel, Vico, Berkeley, and Lessing, as well as literary references to Shakespeare, poet John Dryden, Pico della Mirandola, Dante, William Blake . . . well, it's almost endless—but these scholars also spend time with the minutia of the book, and frankly, I find it fascinating. When I was in Dublin, visiting the Martello tower, I tried to track for my own curiosity just how long it took for Stephen to walk from the tower to the school in Dalkey. Did he walk, or take the train? Was he on time for the class he was teaching, or did he show up late? Dalkey is 1.2 miles from the Martello tower. It took me about 30 minutes to walk it, but I figured Stephen would have made better time than me. When did Stephen leave the tower? At the end of the previous episode, we hear the bells chime, marking the time at quarter hour intervals, so I figured he set out at 8:45 A.M. That means that Stephen got to the classroom around 9:10 A.M. Verdict? Stephen was late for the class he was teaching. Would you like more on this riveting subject? Check out Ian Gunn and Clive Hart's book *Topological Guide to the Dublin of "Ulysses,"* and Jack McCarthy and Danis Rose's *Joyce's Dublin: A Walking Guide to "Ulysses."* Anyway, after the class, Stephen received his pay from the headmaster, an anti-Semitic nationalist who declares that the reason Jews were never oppressed in Ireland was because "we never let them in."

In Episode 3, Stephen walks down to Sandymount Strand, a wide expanse of sand on the edge of Dublin Bay. I've just checked my copies of the two books mentioned above. Shall we once again do the math? It's 1.5 miles from Dalkey to Dublin Bay, figure a 30-minute walk, including the short train ride. Did Stephen get off the train at Lansdowne Station and walk from there, or did he go all the way to the Westland Row Station in town and then make his way to Sandymount Shore? Why should I even care? Because despite all the references and allusions, there is something about *Ulysses* that exists in the imagination more true to life than the most evocative novel. The cast of characters is large, and each character feels real. Joyce also sprinkles Stephen's thoughts with countless references to the "street furniture" of Dublin in 1904. It is often said that if Dublin were to disappear completely, it could be reconstructed from every street, store, pub, and park mentioned in the book.

In the remaining 15 episodes of *Ulysses*, we meet two other Dubliners: Leopold Bloom and his wife, Molly. Both Leopold and Stephen wander about the streets of Dublin throughout the day, crossing paths once in the newspaper office, once while Stephen is giving a lecture on Shakespeare at the National Museum, and at the end of the novel, at Bella Cohen's brothel in "Nightown," where Stephen gets drunk and is kicked out. Bloom helps him sober up, they walk back to Bloom's apartment to share some cocoa, then both take a piss out in the garden under the night sky, above them "the heaventree of stars hung with humid night-blue fruit." Stephen leaves. It's Thursday, June 16th, 1904, the day that's celebrated all over the world as "Bloomsday," the day on which *Ulysses* takes place.

After Stephen leaves, Leopold gets in bed next to Molly, lying head to feet, feet to head, kissing "the plump mellow yellow smellow melons on her rump, plump melonous hemisphere, in their mellow yellow furrow, with obscure prolonged provocative melon-smellonous osculation." The last episode of the novel is Molly Bloom's interior monologue, often called her soliloquy, the most famous episode of the novel, a standalone dramatic piece frequently done theatrically as a one-woman performance. The one I saw in 1977 here in Los Angeles at the Huntington Theater was written by and starred Fionnula Flanagan and directed by Burgess Meredith. In this tribute to James Joyce, Fionnula Flanagan gives a tour-de-force performance as a half-dozen or so women in Joyce's real and fictional worlds. When she portrays his wife Nora remembering their time together, Flanagan captures the era and the author in lyrical detail. As Sylvia Beach, the woman who first published *Ulysses*, new dimensions concerning the importance of Nora in Joyce's literary visions of women emerge, and when Flanagan interprets Joyce characters like Molly Bloom or a washerwoman from *Finnegans Wake*, the beauty of Joyce's language shines through (IMDB). The play was filmed in 1983, released in 1985, with Flanagan both producing and playing all six main female roles—Joyce's wife, Nora Barnacle, as well as fictional characters Molly Bloom, Gerty McDowell, etc. You can also find the film on YouTube under "James Joyce's Women 1985," with Molly Bloom's soliloquy starting around minute 50. The feature film of *Ulysses* was made in 1967, directed by Joseph Strick.

We eloped, all right," Nora Barnacle said, "but didn't get married for 27 years." About her husband, James Joyce, she once said: "He knows nothing about women."

Joyce, age 22, in 1904. Asked what he was thinking about when CP Curran photographed him, Joyce replied, "I was wondering would he lend me five shillings."

So What's the Scoop on Joyce's *Ulysses*?

It's a boring novel. Joyce never even called it a novel; he always referred to it as "the book." The action of the book takes place on one day, Thursday, June 16th, 1904. "Action" is somewhat of an overstatement. There is no significant action, unless you consider Leopold Bloom's farting at the end of Episode 7 as action. There's no big beginning with a plot setup, no big ending with a compelling denoument. Imagine James Joyce pitching the plot to several Suits in a Hollywood producer's office.

"So," Suit One says, "in a nutshell, what's the story?"

"Leopold Bloom," Joyce says, "an Irish-Jew, wanders the streets of Dublin running errands."

"That's it?" Suit Two asks.

"That's it," says Joyce. He sees their puzzled looks, so he carries on, with a little more enthusiasm: "Well, he gets liver from the local butcher shop and comes home and feeds part of it to the cat."

"Is the cat an important character in the book?"

"Everybody's important," says Joyce. "There are a few hundred characters, including the cat, a dog named Tatters, a dead dog, a horse, some cows, a whale, an elephant, a baboon, a badger, a—"

"—How many animals in all?" Suits want to know.

"About 800."

"Okay, never mind the animals, what else does this Bloom fellow do?"

"Then Bloom buys lemon soap for his wife, takes a bath in a local spa, then attends a funeral, and after the funeral he places an ad in a local paper, eats lunch, visits a pub, walks on the beach and masturbates while watching a young girl on the beach, attends a lecture at the National Gallery where our second protagonist, Stephen Dedalus, is giving a lecture on Shakespeare's *Hamlet*, after which Bloom visits another pub where an anti-Semitic "Citizen" throws Bloom out, whereupon he visits a friend in the hospital who is having a baby, then goes to a brothel in "Nighttown," rescues a drunk Stephen Dedalus from two sailors who have beaten him up for blaspheming the honor of the Queen, then brings Stephen back to his apartment where they drink hot cocoa and take a piss out in the back yard, after which Leopold sends Stephen off into the night. It's about two o'clock in the morning. Bloom gets into bed with his wife Molly, whose final soliloquy as Leopold sleeps goes on for 25 pages in a stream-of-consciousness sort of meandering way, ending with the memory of when she and Leopold consummated their love on Howth Heath when he lay atop her and she asked him to ask her again with his eyes if she would consent to sexual intercourse and she responded yes I said yes I will Yes."

"That's the big finish?" Suit Three asks.

"Big Finish," says Joyce.

The book is not what you'd call a page turner. By the time you get to Episode 3, you're going to be befuddled with Stephen's "stream-of-consciousness" as he walks about Sandymount Strand, picking his nose and peeing in the sand. This is where most readers who attempt to read this book wave the white flag and quit reading. If you persevere, you encounter episodes that evoke scenes in Homer's *Odyssey*, though somewhat loosely. For instance, the "Aeolus" Episode 7 features Bloom trying to place an ad in a local newspaper. In the *Odyssey*, Aeolus, a minor Greek god, gave Odysseus a favorable wind and a bag in which the unfavorable winds were confined. Odysseus' companions opened the bag; the winds escaped and drove them back to the island. In the newspaper episode of *Ulysses*, Bloom is beset by doors opening and closing as wind gusts blow papers everywhere, and the editor himself is somewhat of a "blowhard." Slight parallels like this would not be so bad, they are somewhat clever. But each episode of *Ulysses* is written in a different style, either a parody of a particular style, or a style that evokes a motif based on the theme of the episode. For instance, when Bloom visits a friend in the hospital who is giving birth, the entire chapter is written in styles that trace the birth and evolution of the English language from Anglo Saxon to Old English to Middle English to Elizabethan English to 19th century Victorian English to 20th Century Modern English, ending with a parody of Anglo-American English which includes various kinds of slang. Episode 11 takes place in the Ormand Hotel Bar, where two sexy waitresses—nicknamed Bronze and Gold, a reference to the color of their hair—hold court, snapping their garter belts when the clock strikes the hour. It is written in a style that mirrors the technique of musical composition, and features several dozen songs of that era sung by the patrons of the bar while someone accompanies them on the piano. Which episode of the *Odyssey* was Joyce invoking? Why, the "Sirens" episode, of course.

Parallels and motifs abound in the book, and each chapter is a minor tour de force. You don't read *Ulysses*, you encounter it. You butt heads with it. You go to battle with it. You accept the challenge. Forget for a moment how difficult it can be. Okay, I know, it's not your usual "page turner" that you read at the beach on a summer vacation. It's more "another shot of whiskey"-turner; Irish whiskey, to be sure. The book has been called a paragon of difficult and obscure literature. "But," some exclaim in defense, "it champions everyday life!" Others point out, "It's a high water mark of European Modernism!" If you need to, just read it as a work of realism. When Stephen Dedalus gives his lecture on Shakespeare in Episode 9, he points out that Shakespeare portrayed the nature of character, not story or plot. Shakespeare stole most of his plots (except for *The Tempest*, which was thinly based on fanciful books recounting tales of explorers shipwrecked on the shores of the new world). It was character that interested Shakespeare. Stephen quotes the bard: "What a piece of work is man." So think of *Ulysses* as that: a record of the lives and activities of several individuals on one particular day. As

Stephen put it: "Every life is many days, day after day." Joyce accounts not just for the dramatic moments, but characters' particularities. Minor details were fascinating to Joyce, and the precision of detail is a most important aspect of his literary method. Bloom is subjected to perhaps the most detailed scrutiny any fictional character has ever undergone. For his wife Molly, he buys a bar of lemon soap at Sweny's and carries it around with him throughout the day, sitting on it during the carriage ride to the funeral at Glasnevin Cemetery. That bar of soap becomes a talisman. When I was in Dublin, I visited Sweny's (still there) and bought 20 bars. They even asked me to read aloud the passage in *Ulysses* where Bloom buys the soap and has to shift it from one pocket to another during the bumpy ride in the carriage. Now, whenever I soap up in the shower, I think of Leopold, Molly, and Stephen. When Lori and I talk about them, we feel as if we're talking about people we know, our neighbors perhaps. On the other hand, if you need to, you can read the book for the richness of its deep symbolic meaning. You can savor those serious moments that some have characterized as sterile intellectual posturing, but I love intellectual posturing now and then, don't you? So: Is *Ulysses* a kind of Bible, or is it nothing more than a encyclopedia?

Lastly, the book's funny as hell. Those who have made it to the end— Molly Bloom's glorious interior monologue—feel as if they've climbed Mt. Everest and planted a flag on its peak. Is it worth the climb? Ask the millions of readers who gather each year in cities and towns all over the world on June 16th to celebrate the book, sing Irish songs, eat Irish stew, drink Guinness and Irish whiskey, and perform one of the episodes from the book. June 16th, known as "Bloomsday." Is it worth the climb? Answer the question yourself. Dive in. I hope this workbook will help guide you through its most difficult episode, where our protagonist walks along Sandymount Strand, adrift, contemplating his future, looking, perhaps, like Telemachus in the *Odyssey*, for a long-lost father. To some extent, we should keep in mind that at 40, Joyce was looking back at his 20-year-old self, about to embark upon a life-long journey of self-exile. Keep in mind that Joyce was not merely rendering the "stream of consciousness" meanderings of our lost-at-sea protagonist, he was poking fun at him, as well. So, dear reader, if your encounter with Episode 3 leaves you somewhat adrift, share a laugh with Mr. Joyce himself, who chuckled in bed beside his wife Nora as he composed this episode, keeping her awake half the night. And worse come to worst, you can set this workbook aside for later, because truth be told, nothing much actually happens in Episode 3. You can skip it for now and go on to Episode 4, where we meet the other protagonist of Joyce's book, Leopold Bloom, the real Odysseus, latinized as Ulysses, Stephen's soon-to-be-found wandering *pater*, a man free from abstract pretensions, and perhaps the real poet of the novel. Bon Voyage!

Odysseus reunites with Telemachus after 20 years (Image ID: CPBA4G, Ivy Close Images / Alamy Stock Photo)

From the Book Review Archives:

The reviewer for *The New York Times Book Review*, on May 28, 1922, called *Ulysses* the "most important contribution that has been made to fictional literature in the 20th century." That doesn't mean he liked it.

ULYSSES by James Joyce

A few intuitive, sensitive visionaries may understand and comprehend "Ulysses," James Joyce's new and mammoth volume, without going through a course of training or instruction, but the average intelligent reader will glean little or nothing from it—even from careful perusal, one might properly say study, of it—save bewilderment and a sense of disgust. It should be companioned with a key and a glossary like the Berlitz books. Then the attentive and diligent reader would eventually get some comprehension of Mr. Joyce's message.

That he has a message there can be no doubt. He seeks to tell the world of the people that he has encountered in the forty years of sentient existence; to describe their conduct and speech and to analyze their motives, and to relate the effect the "world," sordid, turbulent, disorderly, with mephitic atmosphere engendered by alcohol and the dominant ecclesiasticism of his country, had upon him, an emotional Celt, an egocentric genius, whose chief diversion and keenest pleasure is self-analysis and whose lifelong important occupation has been keeping a notebook in which has been recorded incident encountered and speech heard with photographic accuracy and Boswellian fidelity.

Moreover, he is determined to tell it in a new way. Not in straightforward, narrative fashion, with a certain sequentiality of idea, fact, occurrence, in sentence, phrase and paragraph that is comprehensible to a person of education and culture, but in parodies of classic prose and current slang, in perversions of sacred literature, in carefully metered prose with studied incoherence, in symbols so occult and mystic that only the initiated and profoundly versed can understand—in short, by means of every trick and illusion that a master artificer, or even magician, can play with the English language.

Before proceeding with a brief analysis of *Ulysses*, and comment on its construction and its content, I wish to characterize it. *Ulysses* is the most important contribution that has been made to fictional literature in the twentieth century. It will immortalize its author with the same certainty that *Gargantua and Pantagruel* immortalized Rabelais, and *The Brothers Karamazov* Dostoyevsky. It is likely that there is no one writing English today that could parallel Mr. Joyce's feat, and it is also likely that few would care to do it were they capable. That statement requires that it be said at once that Mr. Joyce has seen fit to use words and phrases that the entire world has covenanted and people in general, cultured and uncultured, civilized and savage, believer and heathen, have agreed shall not be used, and which are base, vulgar, vicious and depraved. Mr. Joyce's reply to this is: "This race and this country and this life produced me—I shall express myself as I am."

He is the only individual that the writer has encountered outside of a madhouse who has let flow from his pen random and purposeful thoughts just as they are produced. He does not seek to give them orderliness, sequence or interdependence. His literary output would seem to substantiate some of Freud's contentions. The majority of writers, practically all, transfer their conscious, deliberate thought to paper. Mr. Joyce transfers the product of his unconscious mind to paper without submitting it to the conscious mind, or, if he submits it, it is to receive approval and encouragement, perhaps even praise. He holds with Freud that the unconscious mind represents the real man, the man of nature, and the conscious mind the artificed man, the man of convention, of expediency, the slave of Mrs. Grundy, the sycophant of the Church, the plastic puppet of society and State. When a master technician of words and phrases sets himself the task of revealing the product of the unconscious mind of a moral monster, a pervert and an invert, an apostate to his race and his religion, the simulacrum of a man who has neither cultural background nor personal self-respect, who can neither be taught by experience nor lessoned by example, as Mr. Joyce has done in drawing the picture of Leopold Bloom, and giving a faithful reproduction of his thoughts, purposeful, vagrant and obsessive, he undoubtedly knew full well what he was undertaking, and how unacceptable the vile contents of that unconscious mind would be to ninety-nine men out of a hundred, and how incensed they would be at having the disgusting product thrown in their faces. But that has nothing to do with that with which I am here concerned, viz., has the job been done well and is it a work of art, to which there can be only an affirmative answer.

Mr. Joyce has no reverence for organized religion, for conventional morality, for literary style or form. He has no conception of the word obedience, and he bends the knee neither to God nor man. It is very interesting, and most important to have the revelations of such a personality, to have them firsthand and not dressed up. Heretofore our only avenues of information of such personalities led through the asylums for the insane, for it was there that such revelations as those of Mr. Joyce were made without reserve. Lest anyone should construe this statement to be a subterfuge on my part to impugn the sanity of Mr. Joyce, let me say at once that he is one of the sanest geniuses that I have ever known.

Finally, I venture a prophecy: Not ten men or women out of a hundred can read *Ulysses* through, and of the 10 who succeed in doing so, five of them will do it as a tour de force. I am probably the only person, aside from the author, that has ever read it twice from beginning to end. I have learned more psychology and psychiatry from it than I did in 10 years at the Neurological Institute. There are other angles at which *Ulysses* can be viewed profitably, but they are not many."

—Dr. Joseph Collins

An American Jesuit on James Joyce's 'Ulysses':

Francis X. Talbot, S.J., was a literary editor of *America: The Jesuit Review*, and editor-in-chief from 1936 to 1944. This year, "in honor of the 100th anniversary of *Ulysses*," the editors of *America: The Jesuit Review* reprinted Talbot's 1934 review of *Ulysses*, which originally appeared twelve years after *Ulysses* was published in 1922, and one year after Judge Woolsey ruled that the book could be distributed and sold in the United States. Joyce took great delight in the negative reviews of his book, and surely, he must have chortled in his joy over this one.

ULYSSES: OBSCENE! BLASPHEMOUS! AGAINST THE NATURAL LAW!

A review by Francis X. Talbot, S.J.

A great pother has been bubbling up for the past twelve years about James Joyce's writings. He tells forlornly in a letter to Dear Mr. Cerf, of Random House, who made a scoop on the sale of American copies of "Ulysses," how he could never get Dublin publishers "to publish anything of mine as I wrote it." No less than twenty-two publishers and printers read the manuscript of "Dubliners," but not one wished to be entangled in the muck. The twenty-second printed it ; one "kind" person bought out the entire edition; and, since it was highly inflammable, the whole edition became burned up. Mr. Joyce arrived in Paris, in 1920, in the summer, with the voluminous manuscript of "Ulysses" and his umbrella. Miss Sylvia Beach, energetic, ran a small English bookshop and lending library, and called herself Shakespeare and Co. Brave, she was braver than professional publishers. Mr. Joyce says: "She took the manuscript and handed it to the printers." The author's eyesight, those eyes which had evidently seen so many sights, permitted him to read the proofs himself. He approved of his work when the first printed copy was presented to him on February 2, in the year 40, James Joyce, otherwise 1922.

The book was written in a new technique, in a pseudo-English, of words that were sometimes normal, sometimes foreign, sometimes archaic, sometimes merely a succession of letters, meaningless and inane. Many of the words were scummy, scrofulous, putrid, like excrement of the mind. The words are listed in the dictionary, but never in the writings or on the tongue of anyone except the insane, or the lowest human dregs.

The critics said how brave. The sexual neurotics said how love-ly. The normal person said I'm sick.

> ## "The book was written in a new technique, in a pseudo-English, of words that were sometimes normal, sometimes foreign, sometimes archaic, sometimes merely a succession of letters, meaningless and inane."

Mr. Joyce used his words to tell what flowed through the minds of three people, Stephen Dedalus, a Dublin man in shabby black and cast-off shoes, Leopold Bloom, a Dublin Jew, and Marion, who was as the reader suspects she was. The flow through their minds continued for twenty-four hours, ac-cording to the Joyce recording; though the events, it may be concluded, summarized twenty-four years. What they and the other characters thought and imagined, what trivialities, what nonsense, what drunken dreams, hallucinations, eroticisms, vulgarities, blasphemies, silliness, malice, and the like streamed through their consciousness and unconsciousness is what James Joyce labored for seven years to transmit to 768 closely printed pages. The poor man, with his own distorted twist of mind, was unable, or did not choose, to express this stream of thought intelligibly. Because of this, the esoteric critics exclaimed what incomparable art. Because of the filthiness that whirled in the stream, those seeking to be pornographicized exclaimed what excitement. And the man with a sound brain and a sound heart exclaimed what twaddle and what rot.

The book sold in Paris, I am told, for forty dollars. And so everybody wished to read it, and a lot of literary fustians wished to write of it. "Ulysses" became internationally famous. It was barred entry into the United States, and that captivated the American imagination and aroused the American curiosity, which curiosity is unequalled the world over. The professional defenders of literary vice exploiters labored indefatigably to spread the mess made by James Joyce before the eyes of all Americans. They arranged a test case which was duly brought before John M. Woolsey, United States District Judge. His de-cision that "'Ulysses' may, therefore, be admitted into the Unit-ed States," rendered December 6, 1933, was hailed ecstatically by Morris L. Ernst, the legal protagonist of literary sexuality, as "the New Deal in the law of letters," as "a major event in the history of the struggle for free expression," as raising Judge Woolsey "to the level of former Supreme Court Justice Oliver Wendell Holmes as a master of juridical prose," and other Oriental exaggerations.

In his Foreword to the American edition of "Ulysses," as in his numerous pleas for unrestricted sexual expression, Mr. Ernst is quite distempered. We who disagree with him have no desire "to emasculate literature." We have not tried "to set up the sensibilities of the prudery ridden as a criterion for society." It is not our aim "to reduce the reading matter of adults to the level of adolescents and subnormal persons," and we have not, at all, "nurtured evasions and sanctimonies." We desire that Mr. Ernst and his authors should not seek "to phallicize literature." We have objected to those who "set up the eroticism of the sex ridden as a criterion for society." It is our aim to withstand those who would wish "to reduce the reading matter of adults to the level of pornographers and neurotic persons." We are opposed to those "nurturing vilenesses and corruptions." Then again, Mr. Ernst devotes a paragraph to a parallel, that "the first week of December, 1933, will go down in history for two repeals, that of Prohibition and that of the legal compulsion for squeamishness in literature." Mr. Ernst's preoccupations would not allow him to see that the Prohibition repeal brought, or was intended to bring back, the pure in alcohol, not the poisonous stuffs. We have never had a Prohibition law against the pure and wholesome in literature. His success through Judge Woolsey has opened the way for the poisonous and the soul killing in literature.

"Lewd and vulgar stories and incidents, with blasphemies that curdle the blood."

But it is not Mr. Ernst, though he is a prime mover in this immoral crusade against decency, that I would discuss. It is Judge Woolsey. In the first place, "Ulysses" was not judged by a jury, but by the Judge alone. His decision is worth what he is worth, only less, under the circumstances. He read the entire book once, and the passages complained of several times; he read its "satellite" books; he gave all his spare time, through several weeks to reading, and thinking. It was a "heavy task."

He was thus equipped by study. Was he equipped in fundamental moralities, was he equipped in psychological perceptiveness, was he equipped with the firm conviction of philosophical thought? He was not guided infallibly; he judged as his personal determinants led him.

The Federal law governing the exclusion of books from this country uses but one word, obscene; State laws employ as many as seven words in their definitions of objectionable books. The word obscene, in Judge Woolsey's determination, which he bases on other decisions, is synonymous with "pornographic, that is, written for the purpose of exploiting obscenity." And that definition, to my mind, is woefully loose; but on it, the Judge rendered his verdict. He strives to analyze the intent of Joyce in writing "Ulysses" as an entirety, and states:

> Joyce has attempted—it seems to me with astonishing success—to show how the screen of consciousness with its ever-shifting kaleidoscopic impressions carries, as it were on a plastic palimpsest, not only what is in the focus of each man's observation of actual things about him, but also in a penumbral zone residua of past impressions, some recent and some drawn up by association from the domain of the subconscious.

Joyce truly attempted this, and, due to the abysmally degraded characters whose consciousness he explored, attempted as an essential part to show how obsessed they were with certain organic functions, with erotic impulses of the lowest nature, with lewd and vulgar stories and incidents, with blasphemies that curdle the blood. These references and sections are the point of issue. These, Judge Woolsey admits, are in the book but excuses as part of the entirety of the recital. I wonder that the loyal Irish have not risen up in violent protest at his summarizing excuse of Joyce: "In respect of the current emergence of the theme of sex in the minds of his characters, it must always be remembered that his locale was Celtic and his season Spring." As if to say, the sex theme is inherent in a Celtic locale.

Judge Woolsey dove into the labyrinthine mind of Joyce, into a crawling diseased mire, as it were, without aid of bathysphere, and rose to the surface with the declaration that Joyce did not intend to exploit obscenity as his primary purpose in his entire 768 pages. Was he intentionally obscene in 100 pages, or fifty pages? If not intentionally, was he actually detailing obscenity in very many specified passages? These, the Judge expurgated from his mind. Yet these, I repeat, are the passages at issue.

"The Monumental Decision" of Judge Woolsey goes on to state that "the meaning of the word obscene as legally defined by the Courts is: tending to stir the sex impulses or to lead to sexually impure and lustful thoughts." He passes, then, from the subjective standard, that of the author's intent, to what he calls a "more objective standard," that is, the result on the minds of readers. He used as a test for this two friends with average sex instincts, "what the French would call *l'homme moyen sensuel*." They reported that the book, in its entirety, did not tend to excite their sexual impulses or lustful thoughts. I can well understand that. But I would like to understand more about these two "assessors." And I would like to have assurance that the thousands who have read and will read "Ulysses" are gauged as they are.

"Only a person who had been a Catholic, only one with an incurably diseased mind, could be so diabolically venomous toward God."

Martin Conboy, United States Attorney, carried the case of "Ulysses" to the United States Court of Appeals. Judges Learned Hand and Augustus N. Hand upheld Judge Woolsey in his opinion. Judge Martin T. Mantón dissented, and declared: "Who can doubt the obscenity of this book after a reading of the passages referred to, which are too indecent to add as a footnote to this account? Its characterization as obscene should be quite unanimous." Mr. Ernst and Judge Woolsey have had their way. Most surprisingly, a Catholic critic of standing most inexplicably pronounces that "we must recognize that Judge Woolsey is right." He states that the Judge "won the approval of authorities both literary and legal." He instances that "the ruling is in harmony with that sound principle of Canon Law, namely, that when the bearing of the law is adverse it is to be given the narrowest possible interpretation." These are three whoopingly misleading statements. I counter them with the simple statement made by one who, in my opinion, is most competent to judge the book: "'Ulysses' is against the natural law."

As far as Catholics are concerned, the case of "Ulysses" is quite clear. Judge Woolsey states that the effect of the book is "emetic;" he does not find it to be "aphrodisiac." It is truly emetic[*]. Our most emetic reactions would be caused not so much by its vulgarity, nor by its indecency, but by its rampant blasphemy. Only a person who had been a Catholic, only one with an incurably diseased mind, could be so diabolically venomous toward God, toward the Blessed Sacrament, toward the Virgin Mary. But the case of "Ulysses" is closed. All the curiosity caused by the extraneous circumstances of its being banned is over. It has now subsided into just a book. It will be discussed, undoubtedly, in the little literary pools of amateurs and young Catholic radicals. But for the most part it is in the grave, odorously.

September 1, 1934

*emetic: a medicine or substance which causes vomiting.

James Joyce met publisher Sylvia Beach in 1920 shortly after he moved to Paris (Bettmann Archive).

A Portrait of *Ulysses* in a Nutshell

PART I

Stephen Dadelus's Self-Exile Begins

- Stephen Dadelus is "usurped" at Martello Tower on Sandycove Point
- Stephen teaches at Dalkey School and gets paid by Mr. Deasy
- Stephen walks on the sand at Sandymount Strand thinking deep thoughts

Stephen has been staying with "stately, plump" Buck Mulligan at the Martello Tower, one of fifty towers built along the eastern coast of Ireland to defend against a threatened Napoleonic invasion. This one is situated on the south Dublin coast at Sandycove Point, located two kilometres to the east of Dun Laoghaire Harbor and 14 kilometres by road from Dublin city center. The entrance was ten feet off the ground, reached by a rope ladder. Now converted to a rental from the War department, the tower had been leased for a year by Stephen for 8£. When Buck asked Stephen for the only key, Stephen feels he has been "usurped," especially by a British character named Haines, a "ponderous Saxon" who scared Stephen in the middle of the night with a nightmare about a panther. It's all too much for Stephen who is grieving his mother's recent death. Stephen goes off to teach at Dalkey Grammar School, a mile's walk from the Tower, and after collecting his pay, he walks on the beach at Sandymont Strand, thinking deep thoughts about thinking deep thoughts, much of it rendered in the style of interior monologue and stream of consciousness, heaven help us.

Episode 1 "Telemachus"
Roomate Buck Mulligan teases him, berates him for not praying at his mother's beside as she was dying. Mulligan and Stephen go down to Sandycove Point for a swim with Haines, their English guest who woke Stephen up with a nightmare about a panther.

Episode 2 "Nestor"
Stephen quizes his students, helps boy with math homework, gets paid by Mr. Deasy, the principal, endures his lecture about saving money, and agrees to bring Deasy's article on foot and mouth disease to a local newspaper.

Episode 3 "Proteus"
Stephen wanders along the beach, recalls time in Paris, note from father "Come home mother dying," contemplates literature, philosophy, life, pees in the sand and picks his nose.

PART II

Leopold Bloom and his Odyssey throughout Dublin

He makes breakfast for Molly, runs errands, buys lemon soap at Sweny's, goes to Paddy Dignam's funeral at Glasnevin Cemetery, tries to place an ad in a newspaper office, stops at a few pubs and places to eat, walks on the shore and masturbates when Gertie MacDonald opens her legs and shows her undergarments, visits the maternity hospital where Mina Purefoy is in labor, goes to a brothel where he encounters a drunken Stephen who has gotten into a fight with three sailors.

Episode 4 "Calypso"
Molly wakes, Bloom makes breakfast, brings mail to Molly, knows she's having a tryst with Blazes Boylan at 4 P.M., leaves to run errands and do business.

Episode 5 "The Lotus Eaters"
Bloom buys lemon soap and lotion for Molly. It's a sleepy morning, he thinks thoughts: the death of their son Rudy a few days after he was born, their lack of intimacy, and a million other things that run through his mind stream of consciousness style, goes to a Turkish bath and as he soaks, watches his pubic hairs rise to the surface of the water, "a languid floating flower."

Episode 6 "Hades"
Bloom rides in the funeral carriage with Simon Dadelus, Martin Cunningham, and Jack Power on their way to Paddy Dignam's funeral at Glasnevin Cemetery. Bloom thinks lots of thoughts and sees a big gray rat in an open grave.

Episode 7 "Aeolus"
Bloom goes to newspaper office trying to place an ad for Keyes, his client, but keeps getting blown off by editor Myles Crawford who tells him to tell Keyes that he can "kiss his bloomin' arse." Stephen shows up to place Deasy's article on hoof and mouth. They make fun of the way Bloom walks.

Episode 8 "The Lestrygonians"
Bloom goes to Burton's for a bite to eat but is repulsed by the eating habits of the men and their stomach-churning crudity. Lots of thoughts of sex, death, and food.

Episode 9 "Scylla and Charybdis"
Bloom sneaks into National Library to avoid being seen by Blazes Boylan and his "white straw hat," where Stephen is giving his lecture on Hamlet following discussion on Aristotle vs Plato with A.E., the poet (George Russell), John Eglinton, essayist, and T.W. Lyster, the Quaker librarian.

Episode 10 "The Wandering Rocks"

central section of the book is composed of nineteen short sections within which most of the characters of *Ulysses* appear, moving about Dublin between 3 P.M. and 4 P.M., set against the background of two overlapping journeys: Father Conmee and the Earl of Dudley's cavalcade.

Episode 11 "The Sirens"

Bloom drops into the Ormand Bar to spy on Blazes Boylan where two charming barmaids, red-haired Miss Lydia Douce and blond Miss Mina Kennedy, "Bronze and Gold" as Joyce labels them, flirt with customers. Lots of singing at the piano.

Episode 12 "The Cyclops"

Bloom goes to Barney Kiernan's pub and encounters The Citizen, a bigoted, racist, anti-Semitic nationalist who wears a patch over one eye and holds court along with his mongrel Gerryowen. After the anti-Semitic rant reaches angry proportions, The Citizen chases Bloom out by throwing a biscuit tin at him and sets Gerryowen to chase after him. Bloom barely escapes in a jarvey car, which Joyce compares to Elijah ascending into Heaven, "amid clouds of angels to the glory of the brightness like a shot off a shovel." This episode is noted for the 30 interpolations or parodies of different rhetorical styles.

Episode 13 "Nausicaa"

Bloom goes to walk on Sandymount Shore and spies Gerty MacDowell, who spreads her legs enough to show Bloom her panties. Bloom reaches into his pocket and masturbates, falls asleep.

Episode 14 "Oxen of the Sun"

Bloom goes by Maternity Hospital where Mina Purefoy is giving another birth while nine medical students, including Buck Mulligan and Stephen Dadelus head out to Burke's Pub, inviting Bloom to join them, which he does. They all get drunk and sing ribald songs, Bloom has a small glass of wine, remains sober.

Episode 15 "Circe"

Bloom, Stephen, and the others end up in Nighttown, Dublin's red-light district, visit Bella Cohen's brothel, where Bloom is dominated and Stephen gets into a fight with several sailors who beat him up before Bloom rescues him.

PART III

Leopold (Father) and Stephen (Son) Return Home.

Leopold helps Stephen by stopping for a late night coffee at a cab stand, Bloom makes some Epps hot-chocolate. After pissing in the garden as they gaze at the starry night sky "hung with a ruby fruit of stars," Bloom offers Stephen the couch to sleep it off, but Stephen declines and disappears into the night. Leopold putters around the kitchen, then clambers into bed with Molly, who's had a tryst with a lover, Blazes Boylan. Leopold brushes away some left-over meat crumbs from the sheet. Lying beside her, head to feet, feet to head, "he kisses the plump yellow smellow melons of her rump." He is home. Ulysses back with his Penelope. He drifts off . . . to sleep. As Leopold sleeps, Molly thinks deep thoughts about her life as a young girl, her marriage to Leopold, and the first time they met and made love when she asked him with her eyes to ask her again and she said yes I said yes I will Yes.

Episode 16 "Eumaeus"
Bloom takes Stephen to a cabman's shelter and sobers him up with coffee.

Episode 17 "Ithaca"
Bloom invites Stephen back to his apartment, they drink hot cocoa, go out and have a piss in the garden looking at the night sky. Stephen wanders off into the night, Bloom retires to bed, lying next to Molly, head to feet, feet to head.

Episode 18 "Penelope"
Molly's soliloquy: Eight long sentences flow like a river in her mind remembering thinking and finally ending with her memory of when she and Bloom first made love on Howth Hill, she asking him to ask her again and her answer: "him as anyone else"—"yes I said yes I will Yes."

McConnell Bridge, Dublin, 1932. "As wide as it is long."

James Joyce: A Portrait of the Author as the Author

"No Mother, let me be and let me live."

James Augustine Aloysius Joyce was born on February 2, 1882, Dublin, Ireland. His masterpiece, *Ulysses*, was published on February 2, 1922, Joyce's 40th birthday. Prior to the book's publication, several chapters, or episodes, had appeared in serialized form in *The Egoist* in England and *The Little Review* in the United States, leading to the confiscation and burning of those issues for obsenity. Thereafter, no publisher or printer in America or England would be responsible for bringing out the complete novel. Finally, Sylvia Beach, owner and proprietor of Shakespeare and Company bookstore in Paris offered to publish it. She had trouble finding a printer who would do the typesetting, since the law against publishing work deemed obscene applied not only to the publisher of note, but the printers as well. A printer in Dijon agreed to do it, and after several drafts and hundreds of revisions at the last minute, the first two copies were bound and sent by train to arrive just in time for Joyce's fortieth birthday. Joyce was noted for his experimental use of language and the exploration of new literary methods in his short stories, *Dubliners* (1914), and in his largely autobiographical novel, *A Portrait of the Artist as a Young Man* (1917), but it was in such large works of fiction as *Ulysses* and *Finnegans Wake* (1939) that Joyce established the modernist techniques for which he is best known, most notably, the technique of "stream of consciousness" (even though Edouard Dejardin and Pamela Richardson had used it first, Joyce extended it beyond their initial tentative efforts). *Ulysses* is considered the most complex linguistic novel of the 20th Century and remains the most influential novel of all time. As a Roman Catholic, Joyce had a complex, critical relationship with the Church, having his alter-ego Stephen Dadelus proclaim that he served three oppressive masters: Ireland, the British government, and the Pope. An early devotion gave way to a deep agnosticism that was yet indebted to the symbolism and structures of Catholicism—and these themes remained a central preoccupation both in his life and in his art. Joyce died on January 13, 1941, in Zürich, Switzerland.

He was the eldest of 10 children in his family to survive infancy and was sent at age six to Clongowes Wood College, a Jesuit boarding school that has been described as "the Eton of Ireland." After his first communion, he becomes an altar boy. He was given four whacks on the back of the hand with a pandybat for use of "vulgar language." But when Joyce was nine, he was removed from Clongowes as the family finances faded. John Joyce lost his job as a Rate Collector and went downhill from there. He was not a man to stay affluent for long; he drank, neglected his affairs, and borrowed money from his office, and his family sank deeper and deeper into poverty, the children becoming accustomed to conditions of increasing sordidness. Joyce did not return to Clongowes in 1891; instead he stayed at home for the next two years and tried to educate himself, asking his mother to check his work. In April 1893 he and his brother Stanislaus were admitted, without fees, to Belvedere College, a Jesuit boys' grammar school in Dublin. Joyce did well there academically and was twice elected president of the Marian Society, a position virtually that of head boy. He left, however, under a cloud, as it was thought (correctly) that he had lost his Roman Catholic faith.

He entered University College, Dublin, which was then staffed by Jesuit priests. There he studied languages and reserved his energies for extracurricular activities, reading widely—particularly in books not recommended by the Jesuits—and taking an active part in the college's Literary and Historical Society. Greatly admiring Henrik Ibsen, he learned Dano-Norwegian so he could read the original and had an article, "Ibsen's New Drama"—a review of the play *When We Dead Awaken*—published in the *London Fortnightly Review* in 1900 just after his 18th birthday. This early success confirmed Joyce in his resolution to become a writer and persuaded his family, friends, and teachers that the resolution was justified. That same year he delivered a paper, "Drama and Life" before the Literary and Historical Society, defending the attention paid to mundane life in contemporary drama (especially Ibsen's). There followed an outraged protest from students who thought he gave short shrift to Irish writers. In October 1901 he published an essay, "The Day of the Rabblement," attacking the Irish Literary Theater (later the Abbey Theater, in Dublin) for its narrow nationalism and for catering to popular taste. Eighty-five copies were privately published in a pamphlet with Francis Skeffington's accompanying essay arguing for equality for women.

Joyce was leading a dissolute life at this time but worked sufficiently hard to pass his final examinations, matriculating with "second-class honours in Latin" and obtaining the degree of B.A. on October 31, 1902. Never did he relax his efforts to master the art of writing. He wrote verse and prose plays, poems, and experimented with short prose passages that he called "epiphanies," a word that Joyce used to describe his accounts of moments when the real truth about some person or object was revealed. To support himself while writing, he decided to become a doctor, but, after attending a few lectures in Dublin, he borrowed what money he could and went to Paris, where he abandoned the idea of medical studies, wrote some book reviews, and studied in the Sainte-Geneviève Library.

Recalled home in April 1903 because his mother was dying, he tried various occupations, including teaching, and lived at various addresses, including the Martello Tower at Sandycove (the tower, still there, has been turned into a Joyce museum). He had begun writing a lengthy naturalistic novel, *Stephen Hero*, based on the events of his own life, when in 1904 George Russell offered £1 each for some simple short stories with an Irish background to appear in a farmers' magazine, *The Irish Homestead*. In response, Joyce began writing short stories, three of which were published in the *Homestead*, and spurred on by his literary success, not to mention the modest payment, he wrote twelve more stories over the course of the next few years. It took several more years to find a publisher for the book, but eventually, fifteen of the stories were published as *Dubliners*. Three stories—"The Sisters," "Eveline," and "After the Race"—had appeared under the pseudonym Stephen Dedalus before the editor decided that Joyce's work was not suitable for his readers. Meanwhile, Joyce had met Nora Barnacle in June 1904; they probably had their first date, and first sexual encounter (though not intercourse), on June 16, the day that he chose for his "circadian novel" *Ulysses*, and the day that is now celebrated around the world as "Bloomsday," referring to the book's ostensible protagonist, Leopold Bloom.

*Outside Pound's studio in the Rue des Champs, Autumn 1923, a year after publication of **Ulysses**. L to R: James Joyce, seated; Ezra Pound, standing, the first volume of his **Cantos**, generally considered one of the most significant works of modernist poetry in the 20th Century, had just been published; Ford Madox Ford, seated, author of the **Parade's End** tetrology and **The Good Solider**, included among Modern Library's "100 Greatest Novels of All Time"; John Quinn, seated, the New York lawyer who effectively was Joyce's representative in America, fighting to overturn censorship laws restricting modern literature and art from entering the United States. Quinn was known for his generosity to Irish artists, acting somewhat as a patron by buying manuscripts of their work, including early handwritten episodes of **Ulysses**, as well as the first draft of T.S. Eliot's "The Waste Land," which included Pound's editorial suggestions. The extent of his generosity and influence was kept secret, revealed only after his death*

James Joyce, Ezra Pound, John Quinn, and Ford Madox Ford, Paris, 1923.

A Digression on Circadian Novels

Circadian novels fit all their action into a single day, all its events squeezed into one 24-hour period. *Ulysses* is probably the most famous and greatest such novel, set in 1904 Dublin on what has come to be known as "Bloomsday," June 16th. The protagonist, Leopold Bloom, mostly wanders the streets of his city: attending a funeral, arguing in a pub, and so on. Another famous circadian novel is *Mrs Dalloway* (1925) by Virginia Woolf, published three years after *Ulysses*. On this average day in London the title character, high-society housewife Clarissa Dalloway, quietly ponders her life as she plans a grand party. Michael Cunningham's *The Hours* (1998), a deliberate homage to Mrs. Dalloway, similarly takes place on one day, while Woolf's *Between the Acts* (1941) is another example of a circadian novel. When Woolf read part of *Ulysses*, she was distinctly sniffy about it, saying it was the work of a frustrated man who felt that, in order to breathe, he had to break all the windows. Perhaps sensing that Joyce might have surpassed her own portrayals of quotidian consciousness, she denounced *Ulysses* as the work of a "queasy undergraduate scratching his pimples," but it gave her the idea for her own day-in-the-life novel, where an MP's wife, Clarissa Dalloway, oversees preparations for a party, wanders around central London, and finally entertains her guests. Time is marked by the chimes of Big Ben.

Nicola Yoon's *The Sun Is Also a Star* is an example of a circadian novel where the main action (except flashbacks, for instance) takes place all on one day. *The Sixteenth of June* (2014) by Maya Lang recreates the format of *Ulysses* in a near-contemporary story set in Philadelphia. *Seize the Day* by Saul Bellow has its main character weeping at a stranger's funeral that he has attended by mistake. In the space of a single day, Bellow's shambling anti-hero Tommy Wilhelm, a failed actor who has lost his job and his wife and has broken relationships with his children and father, reviews his life and his failures. The great Russian dissident, Alexander Solzhenitsyn had the grimmest reason to stay within the frame of a single day in his *One Day in the Life of Ivan Denisovich*. His alter ego lives through one more day of suffering in one of Stalin's gulags, every minute an ordeal, with no end in sight. This day is all he knows and is his prison. *Saturday,* by Ian McEwan, starts in the early hours of one night, as the neurosurgeon protagonist Henry Perowne is woken by an ominous burning object in the skies, and ends at just the same time on the next night, with our hero completing a risky brain operation. All this, even though it is his day off. *Intimacy* by Hanif Kureishi, is also more night than day. We start in the evening, with Kureishi's narrator planning to leave his family. While he obeys the usual domestic rhythms—a glass of wine with his wife, bedtime rituals with the children—we hear what he is really thinking and planning. In the morning, he leaves. Rachel Cusk's novel, *Arlington Park*, has satirical reasons for staying within circadian confines. The women who live in the suburb of Arlington Park are trapped in lives of unquiet desperation, and the daily routine that the novel itself follows is what drives them maddest. For most of the novel the men are off at work, but there's no escape from the children. And today it's raining. All these novels owe, in one way or another, a debt to Joyce's *Ulysses*.

Joyce and Woolf are known for their stream-of-consciousness style; that's certainly not an essential element, though many circadian narratives are in the present tense to capture a sense of immediacy. Literary critic John Mullan believes that the first true circadian novel was *Twice Round the Clock* (1859) by George Augustus Sala, a protégé of Charles Dickens. It devotes one chapter to each hour of the day and includes vivid descriptions of everyday meals and fashion in 1850s London. The circadian novel was popular through the twentieth century. Other twentieth-century books set on one day include *Under the Volcano* (1947) by Malcolm Lowry, *Billiards at Half-Past Nine* (1959) by Heinrich Boll, *A Single Man* (1964) by Christopher Isherwood, *Do Androids Dream of Electric Sheep?* (1968) by Philip K. Dick, *Hogfather* (1996) by Terry Pratchett, *Cosmopolis* (2003) by Don DeLillo, and *After Dark* (2004) by Haruki Murakami.

The events of 9/11 seemed to spark new interest in the circadian novel, reminding readers of how much difference one day can make. *Eleven* (2006) by David Llewelyn, is set on 9/11 itself and told through emails sent around a financial office in Wales. Other 2000s novels set on one day include *Mr. Phillips* (2000) by John Lanchester. The accountant protagonist of Lanchester's solemnly funny tale sets out for work on a day like any other. Except that he has lost his job, and his day will be a bizarrely eventful wander around London, his mind upon sex and statistics. Like several circadian novels, it is in the present tense. Another such novel is *Intimacy* (2001) by Hanif Kureishi, *The Light of Day* (2003) by Graham Swift. George Webb, private detective, marks a special day, the anniversary of a murder that has changed his life. And he visits the murderer, a woman with whom he has fallen in love. Swift is very keen on this form, which he has used three or four times. His last novel, *Tomorrow*, spanned a single night.

Circadian narratives have been particularly popular in young adult fiction. A few years ago Book Riot published a list of YA circadian novels with no fewer than 13 examples, such as *Forgive Me, Leonard Peacock* (2013) by Matthew Quick. Nicola Yoon's second book thus takes its place in a crowd of fun, fast-paced novels that reflect the teenage experience of momentous days.

Other novels that take place in a 24-hour period are: *French Lessons* by Ellen Sussman; *A Single Man* by Christopher Isherwood; *Man in the Dark* by Paul Auster; *On Chesil Beach* by Ian McEwan; *Run* by Ann Patchett; *Dear American Airlines* by Jonathan Miles; *Embers* by Sandor Marai; *The Following Story* by Cees Nooteboom; *If Nobody Speaks of Remarkable Things* by Jon McGregor; *Vox* by Nicholson Baker; *Vertical Run* by Joseph R. Garber; *Odd Thomas* by Dean Koontz; *Molly Fox's Birthday* by Deidre Madden; *Next* by James Hynes; *Where Are The Children?* by Mary Higgins Clark; *The Life and Opinions of Tristam Shanty, Gentleman* by

Laurence Sterne; *Last Night at the Lobster* by Stewart O'Nan; *Blast From the Past* by Ben Elton; *Windows on the World* by Frederic Beigbeder; *Death of a River Guide* by Richard Flanagan; *The Reluctant Fundamentalist* by Mohsin Hamid; *The Colorado Kid* by Stephen King; and *The Almost Moon* by Alice Sebold.

Myriams-Fotos, 2017

The Famine Memorial in Dublin Ireland is a collection of statues designed and crafted by Dublin sculptor Rowan Gillespie and presented to the city of Dublin in 1997.

The Tale of the Wandering Irishman Continues

Eventually Joyce persuaded Nora to leave Ireland with him, although he refused, on principle, to go through a ceremony of marriage. This fact was concealed from his parents, and Nora boarded the ship for France separately from Joyce, but at the last minute, Joyce's uncle noticed Nora, figured out what was going on, and revealed the truth to his parents as the ship set sail. They left Dublin together in October 1904.

Joyce obtained a position in the Berlitz School at Pola in Austria-Hungary (now Pula, Croatia), while working in his spare time at his novel and short stories. In 1905 they moved to Trieste, where James's brother Stanislaus joined them and where their children, Georgio and Lucia, were born. In 1906–07, for eight months, he worked at a bank in Rome, disliking almost everything he saw. Ireland seemed pleasant by contrast; he wrote to Stanislaus that he had not given credit in his stories to the Irish virtue of hospitality and began to plan a new story, "The Dead." The early stories were meant, he said, to show the stultifying inertia and social conformity from which Dublin suffered, but they were written with a vividness that arose from his success in making every word and every detail significant. His studies in European literature had interested him in both the Symbolists and the realists of the second half of the 19th century; his work began to show a synthesis of these two rival movements. He decided that his novel *Stephen Hero* lacked artistic control and form, so he scrapped the twenty-six chapters already written, and rewrote it as "a work in five chapters" under a title—*A Portrait of the Artist as a Young Man*—intended to direct attention to its focus upon the central figure.

In 1909 he visited Ireland twice to try to publish *Dubliners*, and once, with the financial backing of several "entrepreneurs" from Trieste, he endeavored to set up a chain of Irish cinemas. Neither effort succeeded, and he was distressed when a former friend told him that he had shared Nora's affections in the summer of 1904. Another old friend proved this to be a lie. Joyce always felt that he had been betrayed, however, and the theme of betrayal runs through much of his later writings.

When Italy declared war in 1915 Stanislaus was interned, but Joyce and his family were allowed to go to Zürich. At first, while he gave private lessons in English and worked on the early chapters of *Ulysses*—which he had first thought of as another short story about a "Mr. Hunter"—his financial difficulties were great. He was helped by a large grant from Edith Rockefeller McCormick and finally by a series of anonymous grants from Harriet Shaw Weaver, editor of the *Egoist* magazine, which by 1930 had amounted to more than £23,000. Her generosity resulted partly from her admiration for his work and partly from her sympathy with his difficulties, for, as well as poverty, he had to contend with eye diseases that never really left him. From February 1917 until 1930 he endured a series of 25 operations for iritis, glaucoma, and cataracts, sometimes being for short intervals totally blind. Despite this he kept up his spirits and continued working, some of his most joyful passages being composed when his health was at its worst.

Unable to find an English printer willing to set up *A Portrait of the Artist as a Young Man* for book publication, Weaver published it herself, having the sheets printed in the United States, where it was also published, on December 29, 1916, by B.W. Huebsch, in advance of the English Egoist Press edition. Encouraged by the acclaim given to this, in March 1918, the American *Little Review* began to publish episodes from *Ulysses*, continuing until the work was banned in December 1920.

An autobiographical novel, *A Portrait of the Artist as a Young Man* traced the intellectual and emotional development of Stephen Dedalus and ended with his decision to leave Dublin for Paris to devote his life to art. The last words of Stephen prior to his departure are thought to express the author's feelings upon the same occasion in his own life:

> Welcome, O life! I go to encounter for the millionth time the reality of experience and to forge in the smithy of my soul the uncreated conscience of my race.

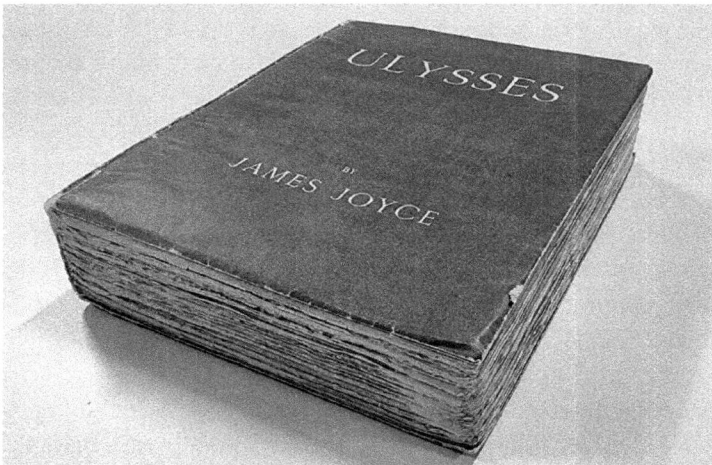

Ulysses was first published in book form in Paris on February 2, 1922. Many readers were baffled by the "stream of consciousness" text, others proclaimed that the book contained a "great deal of unmitigated filth and obscenity." Officials in the United Kingdom and the United States demanded that the book be kept out of the country under a law prohibiting the importation of indecent items. By April 1923, they began seizing and destroying shipments of the book. With a few narrow exceptions, Ulysses remained banned for more than a decade. In 1933 a U.S. court decision removed the ban. In the UK, officials acknowledged changing standards and the ban was quietly removed. In 1934, Random House Modern Library issued the first edition to be sold in the United States. In 1936, the Bodley Head of London issued the first printing of 1,000 copies, of which the first 100 were signed by the author. Photo of 1922 first edition, first printing via Wikimedia Commons.

The Book

After World War I Joyce returned for a few months to Trieste, and then—at the invitation of Ezra Pound—in July 1920 he went to Paris. His novel *Ulysses* was published there on February 2, 1922, by Sylvia Beach, proprietor of the bookshop Shakespeare and Company. *Ulysses* is constructed as a modern parallel to Homer's *Odyssey*. All of the action of the novel takes place in Dublin on a single day (June 16, 1904). The three central characters—Stephen Dedalus (the hero of Joyce's earlier *Portrait of the Artist*), Leopold Bloom, and his wife, Molly Bloom—are intended to be modern counterparts of Telemachus, Odysseus [Latinized as Ulysses], and Penelope. By the use of interior monologue, Joyce reveals the innermost thoughts and feelings of these characters as they live hour by hour, waking, making breakfast, running errands at various Dublin shops, walking on the beach at Sandymont Shore, teaching a grammar school class, visiting, a public bath, attending a funeral, having drinks and lunch in several pubs, giving lectures at the National Library of Dublin, having a late afternoon snack at a hotel bar, going for another walk on the beach, attending the birth of a friend's son at a maternity hospital, then going to a brothel, getting stinking drunk, and trying to sober up at a late-night cab stand, after which our two wayfarers finish their odyssey by making it home to Bloom's place. After sharing a cup of Epps cocoa, and enjoying a backyard piss under the "heaventree of stars," Stephen heads out and Bloom crawls into bed with his wife, Molly Bloom. The book concludes with Molly's interior monologue—thoughts as she lies in bed, recalling, among other things, her childhood in Gibralter, her sexual encounters, the death of their child eleven days after he was born, the fact that she and Leopold hadn't been intimate since Rudy's death, and her resolve to give Leopold one more chance, that she would do her best to entice him into sex by encouraging his fantasies. Her monologue concludes with the famous lines, remembering the first time they made love on Howth Head:

> . . . . yes and those handsome Moors all in white and turbans
> like kings asking you to sit down in their little bit of a shop
> and Ronda with the old windows of the posadas glancing eyes
> a lattice hid for her lover to kiss the iron and the wineshops
> half open at night and the castanets and the night we missed
> the boat at Algeciras the watchman going about serene with
> his lamp and O that awful deepdown torrent O and the sea
> the sea crimson sometimes like fire and the glorious sunsets
> and the figtrees in the Alameda gardens yes and all the queer
> little streets and pink and blue and yellow houses and the rose-
> gardens and the jessamine and geraniums and cactuses and Gi-
> bralter as a girl where I was a Flower of the mountain yes when
> I put the rose in my hair like the Andalusian girls used or shall

I wear a red yes and how he kissed me under the Moorish wall and I thought well as well him as another and then I asked him with my eyes to ask again yes and then he asked me would I yes to say yes my mountain flower and first I put my arms around him yes and drew him down to me so he could feel my breasts all perfume yes and his heart was going like mad and yes I said yes I will Yes."

The main strength of *Ulysses* lies in its depth of character portrayal and its breadth of humor. Yet the book is most famous for its use of a variant of the interior monologue known as the stream-of-consciousness technique. Joyce claimed to have taken this technique from a largely forgotten French writer, Édouard Dujardin, who had used interior monologues in his novel *Les Lauriers Sont Coupés* (1888); [English translation: *We'll to the Woods No More*], but many critics have pointed out that interior monologue is at least as old as the novel, though no one before Joyce had used it so continuously. Joyce's major innovation was to carry the interior monologue one step further by rendering, for the first time in literature, the myriad flow of impressions, half thoughts, associations, images, lapses and hesitations, incidental worries, and sudden impulses that form part of the individual's conscious awareness along with the trend of his rational thoughts. This "stream-of-consciousness" technique proved widely influential in much 20th-century fiction. The terms "interior monologue" and "stream-of-consciousness" are often confused and used interchangeably. There's a significant difference, though, in presenting the silent thoughts of a character, in normal sentences, as if the character were saying them aloud in her head, and presenting the complex nature of consciousness in the literary convention of half-sentences, disconnected images, phrases, and incoherent associations. By literary "convention," we mean a technique that is meant to represent what cannot ultimately be represented in a work of art because consciousness is more complex than the linear process of speaking or thinking. Reading a written text is linear. Thinking thoughts—one after the other—is linear. But consciousness is holistic. Everything happens in the mind at once: thoughts, images, associations, sensations, etc.

The technical and stylistic devices in *Ulysses* are abundant, particularly in the much-praised "Oxen of the Sun" chapter (Episode 14), which takes place at the Holles Street Maternity Hospital where Leopold Bloom has gone to check in on Mrs. Purefoy, who has been in labor for three days. In the course of this episode, the language goes through every stage in the development of English prose from Anglo-Saxon to present day slang, symbolizing the growth of a fetus in the womb. The effect of these devices is often to add intensity and depth, as, for example, in the "Aeolus" chapter (Episode 7), based on the episode in the *Odyssey* in which the ship's crew opens the bag of winds, releasing them, thus blowing Odysseus's ship off course. Joyce sets the "Aeolus" episode in a newspaper office, with rhetoric as the theme. Joyce inserted into this chapter hundreds of rhetorical figures and many references to winds—something "blows up" instead of happening, people "raise the wind" when they are getting money—and the reader becomes aware of an unusual liveliness in the very texture of the prose. The editor himself, Myles Crawford, is always shouting and yelling—he's portrayed as something of a "blowhard" or a "windbag." The famous last chapter of the novel, in which we follow the stream of consciousness of Molly Bloom as she lies in bed, gains much of its effect from being written in eight huge, unpunctuated paragraphs, except for the middle sentence, which ends in a period, and the last sentence, which ends with her memory of consenting to have sex with Leopold and answering his entreaty with the capitalized word "Yes" and a very large period. "yes I said yes I will Yes." We ride the thoughts and associations of Molly Bloom as if we were being tossed about in a small boat descending the rapids, not just a "stream" of consciousness, but a white water river.

Joyce never referred to *Ulysses* as a novel. He always called it "the book." It was already well-known because of the censorship troubles and became immediately famous upon publication. Its critical reception was anticipated even before publication. Valery Larbaud, French critic and author, gave a lecture at a left-bank bookstore, *La Maison des Amis des Livres*, to a packed crowd. He pointed out the Homeric correspondences in it, that each episode had its own specific narrative technique, and "each episode deals with a particular art or science, contains a particular symbol, represents a special organ of the human body, has its particular colour, proper technique, and takes place at a particular time." Joyce never published this scheme; indeed, he even deleted the chapter titles in the book as printed. It's important to remember that the schema was drawn up after the book was completed, but was not necessarily a blueprint that Joyce consulted each time he sat down to write. Perhaps he had a notion of the schema, since he was quite familiar with Homer's *Odyssey* anyway. It's not as if he had to write it down. Whether written as a reference guide or something he saw in his mind beforehand, such scheme was probably more useful to Joyce when he was writing *Ulysses* than it is to the reader today, but I must admit, while I may not rely on the different correspondences for every technique, I find the titles useful and easy to connect to the subject of the episode in mind. "Penelope" is Molly's soliloquy, "Aeolus" is the windy newspaper offices, "Hades" is the funeral in Glasnevin Cemetery, "Sirens" is the Ormand Bar with the two barmaids Bronze and Gold. Easy to remember and easy to make sense of. Joyce sent a diagram for the novel a year before its publication to help his friend, Stuart Gilbert, understand the fundamental structure of the book. The first substantial critical work devoted to *Ulysses* was Gilbert's 1930 book, *James Joyce's "Ulysses": A Study*, which included the schema Joyce had sent him. This schema was a version of the one Joyce had sent Larbaud in 1921, but the two are not exactly the same. There's another version of the schema that Joyce sent to the Italian critic Carlo Linati. That one differs markedly in some respects from the ones he sent Larbaud and Gilbert. The original copy of the Gilbert schema is housed in the Harley K. Croessmann Collection of James Joyce at Southern Illinois University Carbondale.

To many of Joyce's early readers, Gilbert's diagram came as something of a shock. But going back over what they had read, many found it added to their appreciation of the whole. When Joyce chose to remove the Homeric titles from his chapters, perhaps he assumed the reader would still experience the correspondences, but most did not make the connection. Joyce talked about the parallels to Homer's *Odyssey* in private conversation, which may have given him a false sense of the obviousness of it. In his wanderings about the streets of Dublin, running errands and conducting business, Leopold Bloom moved along a north-westerly axis, just as Odysseus did through the Mediterranean working his way back to Ithaca, but this parallel was not readily obvious to the general reader, or to many of the critics. Knowing that Episode 12 paralleled the Cyclops episode in the *Odyssey* heightens the humor of the scene in Barney Kiernan's pub when Bloom shakes a cigar at the chauvinist citizen, almost putting his eye out, just as Odysseus launched a burning stake of olive wood and blinded the Cyclops. Joyce's penchant for comedy turns this episode into both a fearful anti-Semitic drama and a hilarious spoof of the actions of the Citizen and his coharts. The 2001 film *O, Brother Where Art Thou?* is also loosely based on the *Odyssey*: George Clooney is a ragged Odysseus, escaping from a chain gang in 1930s Mississippi with his crew of John Turturro and Tim Blake Nelson. There are many parallels to the *Odyssey*, including the blind railroad conductor who prophesizes the future of the main characters, just as Tiresias prophesizes the future of Odysseus and his crew in the "Land of the Dead" episode. The characters disguise themselves as KKK members to free Tommy, just as Odyseus and his crew hide under the sheep to escape from Polyphemus. Big Dan T, played by John Goodman wearing a black eye-patch over one eye, dies by the flaming wooden cross. Odyseus tells King Alcinos of his journey home, just as the characters sing about their lives on a local radio station. The film is enjoyable even without knowing the parallels, but becomes more so when the viewer makes the connections. The same is true for Joyce's *Ulysses*. Some critics objected to the schema, claiming it was merely the scaffolding used to construct the novel, and once finished, the scaffold should be taken away. But I disagree. We can enjoy a great dish served for dinner without knowing the recipe, but there are those who find even greater pleasure in appreciating the recipe, being able to discern, perhaps, the suggestion of tarragon or the subtle taste of the cabernet sauvignon the meat was cooked in, the slice of apple to give it that sweeter tang. We ask the host for the recipe, which allows us to enjoy the meal even more. The yoking of an ancient saga to a modern novel functions as more than scaffolding in Joyce's

Ulysses. Sometimes there is the love of analogy for its own sake, but more often the parallels enhance the scenes and either gives them greater magnitude or supplies a counter-balance of humor. In most cases, Joyce's analogies scale the grandiose heroic images of the *Odyssey* down to a human dimension, as if he were domesticating the epic. Leopold Bloom is not the cunning warrior inflicting suffering on his enemies. Rather, his heroism manifests itself in his ability to endure. Odysseus slaughters the suitors who've come to take his wife. Bloom takes no physical vengeance on the man who cuckolded him. His victories are mental, psychological, emotional. As Yeats said in his later years, a man may show greater bravery and courage by "entering the abyss of himself." Joyce's *Ulysses* is an epic of the mind. As readers, we are transported along the flow of that stream of consciousness that accompanies the trivial events of the day, the mundane moments filled with objects, like the lemon soap in Bloom's pocket or the throwaway paper that others mistake for a suggestion to bet on the horse "Throwaway" in the Gold Cup race being run that day, an ordinary day in the life of several dozen Dubliners. In the penultimate episode when Bloom returns home at two o'clock in the morning, standing in the yard peeing as he and Stephen look up at the "heaventree of stars hung with humid nightblue fruit," the bells in the church of Saint George peal the hour. Stephen hears *Liliata rutilantium. Turma circumdet. Iubilantium te virginum. Chorus excipiat.* Bloom hears *Heighho, heigho. Heighho, heigho.*

> *Where were the several members of the company which with Bloom that day at the bidding of that peal had traveled from Sandymount in the south to Glasnevin in the north?*
>
> Martin Cunningham (in bed), Jack Power (in bed), Simon Dedalus (in bed), Tom Kernan (in bed), Ned Lambert (in bed), Joe Hynes (in bed), John Henry Menton (in bed), Bernard Corrigan (in bed), Patsy Dignam (in bed), Paddy Dignam (in the grave).
>
> *Alone, what did Bloom feel?*
>
> The cold in interstellar space, thousands of degrees below freezing point or the absolute zero of Fahrenheit, Centigrade or Réaumur: the incipient intimations of proximate dawn.
>
> *How?*
>
> With circumspection, as invariably when entering an abode (his own or not his own): with solicitude, the snakespiral springs of the mattress being old, the brass quoits and pendent viper radii loose and tremulous under stress and strain: prudnetly, as entering a lair or ambush of lust or adder: lightly, the less to disturb: reverently, the bed of conception and of birth, of

consummation of marriage and of breach of marriage, of sleep and death.

Then?

He kissed the plump mellow yellow smellow melons of her rump, on each plump melonous hemishphere, in their mellow yellow furrow, with obscure prolonged provacative melon-smellonous osculation ●

*Barbara Jefford as Molly Bloom in 1967 film **Ulysses**, a Ulysses Film Production. Licensed from Alamy.*

Episode 3, "Proteus": Summary & Overview

Stephen on Sandymount Strand

Stephen, the dreamer, takes a stroll on Sandymount Strand.
He imagines he's blind and taps along with his ashplant (cane).
"Ineluctable modality of the visible: at least that if no more,
thought through my eyes. Signature of all things I am here to
read, seaspawn and seawrack, the nearing tide, that rusty boot."
He thinks about his writing career and his dead mother. He
vividly recalls memories of his recent stay in Paris. Imagination
enfolds him, as nearly does the turning tide. Across the expan-
sive sand a dog bounds. Our bard has a stab at writing a poem,
pees in the sand, and picks his nose.

"Ineluctable"—that from which one cannot escape even by struggling—fittingly
opens this episode, titled "Proteus," thereby naming it after the endlessly mutat-
ing sea god forced into fixed form by the "ineluctable" Menelaus from Homer's
Odyssey who discovered that Proteus possessed the gift of prophecy but that he
must be held fast before he will speak. If caught, he will foretell the future. Since
Proteus can assume "the shape of every creature that moves on earth, and of water and of portentous fire," catching him is very difficult. Fixity and flux, space
and time, actuality and imagination: these are the twin poles between which this
dense and difficult-to-follow episode moves. Stephen, after Aristotle, regards
the material world—space—as "what you damn well have to see."

Don't forget, like Joyce himself, Stephen's eyesight is severely impaired,
limiting what he can see, and that includes his future, both the near-term—
where will he sleep tonight, will he still have a job?—and the long-term—does
he remain in Dublin, in a state of artistic paralysis and literary parochialism,
or does he opt for self-exile in Paris, Rome, or Trieste? Stephen is lost and in
despair. The other difficulty of this episode lies in Joyce's narrative strategy, os-
cillating from third-person omniscient to first person interior monologue with
subtle shifts into stream of consciousness. Thus, Stephen transforms the material world around him through mental acts of speculation. Here, Stephen plays
simultaneously the parts of speculator and spectator (both of which have their
roots in the Latin *specere*, "see, look."). One problem for the reader comes in trying
to sort out when he is playing which—the spectator or the speculator. For, with
only a handful of sentences excepted, the narrative proceeds through Stephen's
interior monologue without the third-person narrator signaling the reader that
"Stephen thought . . . ." The shift from third person "he" to first person "I" occurs
without any attribution, so the shifts occur almost as fast as Proteus shifts forms,
and just as fast as thought and sight interweave. Furthermore, Stephen's interior
monologue is prompted by what he sees, and what he sees is dependent upon

what he thinks. If there is any episode in *Ulysses* that could cause the reader to get whiplash, this is it. No other episode in *Ulysses* is this radical in its use of interior monologue *and* stream of consciousness combined. Even Molly Bloom's long eight-sentence monologue that ends the novel is easy by comparison. In fact, Molly's thoughts are all interior monologue, thoughts that she's speaking as run-on-sentences in her mind; but in this episode, Joyce manipulates the narrative by weaving together the devices of interior monologue *and* stream of consciousness, which are different, but often used by many critics incorrectly interchangeably. (I just inherited a lot of money so I can afford those two adverbs one after the other.)

As he walks, thinks, sits, writes a poem, pisses, and picks his nose, Stephen observes two midwives, the sea, sand, boulders, a man and a woman cocklepicking, a dead dog, a live dog, his shadow, Cock lake, no black clouds, and a three-masted ship moving across the harbor. His thoughts are more active and carry him back to fourteenth-century Dublin, sixteenth-century Denmark, seventeenth-century London; to the words of heretics, philosophers, Renaissance writers, contemporary poets, and French historians; to memories of visits to his aunt Sara's; of sighting a woman outside Hodges Figgis bookstore who flashes her undergarments; of conversations with the "wild goose" Kevin Eagan when he was in Paris before his mother died; of his own adolescent writerly pretensions; of an early morning dream; to imagined sightings of drowned corpses and imagined enactment of the role of Hamlet and Acteon (in his stag form). Matter, space, time, all mutate in response to Stephen's thoughts.

While Stephen likes looking and freely transforming the spectacle in his mind, he is himself frequently anxious that he, himself, might be seen. "Who watches me here?"; "Can't see who's behind me?" (This sense of an unseen person following behind recurs throughout the novel, not just to Stephen, but to Bloom as well.) For he is much happier as spectator than as spectacle, and his transformations of matter, derived as they are from his acts of seeing, place him in the position of power as the subject, not the object, of the gaze. In his early experiment ("Shut your eyes and see") Stephen attempts to determine whether space is dependent on his perceiving it. His admission that the world exists "there all the time without you" ("without": both "independently of" and "outside") corresponds to his earlier thoughts (in the previous episode) that historical figures and events are not to be "thought away."

Still, he unhappily inhabits the position of object just as he persistently resents his existence as matter. Note how he identifies himself with his father's voice, his ended shadow, Aristotle's "soul . . . form of forms"—all insubstantial entities. Just so, the *lex eterna* [eternal law]. . . " wherein Father and Son are consubstantial." Matter means mortality, a body which can become "a bag of corpsegas" through whose "buttoned trouserfly" minnows may flit and grow fat in eating "a spongy titbit." However much Stephen accepts the material existence of the world and its cycles of birth and death, he prefers the regeneration more easily accomplished in the artist's imagination. But as Stephen Dogsbody (as Buck Mulligan has named him) speculates, live dog "moves to one great goal . . . poor dogsbody's body." That much is ineluctable, inescapable.

In this episode, Stephen walks on the beach, contemplating the difference between the material world as it exists and as it is registered by his eyes. Stephen closes his eyes and lets his hearing take over—rhythms emerge. Opening his eyes, Stephen notices two midwives, Mrs. Florence MacCabe and another woman. Stephen imagines that one has a miscarried fetus in her bag. He imagines an umbilical cord as a telephone line running back through history through which he could place a call to "Edenville." Stephen pictures Eve's navel-less stomach. He considers woman's original sin, and then his own conception. Stephen contrasts his own conception with that of Christ. According to the Nicene Creed, a part of the Catholic mass, Christ was "begotten, not made," meaning that he is part of the same essence as God the Father and was not made by God the Father out of nothing. Stephen, in contrast, was "made not begotten," in that though he has biological parents, his soul was created out of nothing and bears no relation to his father's. Stephen would like to argue the specifics of divine conception (are the Father and the Son the same being or not?) with heretic-scholars of the past.

The sea air blows upon him, and Stephen remembers that he must take Deasy's letter about cattle's foot and mouth disease to the newspaper, then meet Buck (stately, plump Buck Mulligan) at The Ship pub at 12:30. He considers turning off the beach to visit his aunt Sara. He imagines his father's mocking reaction to such a visit (his father is disgusted by his brother-in-law, Richie, who is Sara's husband). Stephen imagines the scene if he were to visit: Richie's son Walter would let him in and uncle Richie, who has back trouble, would greet Stephen from bed.

Coming out of his reverie, Stephen remembers feeling ashamed of his family when he was a child. This disgust for his family brings Jonathan Swift to mind—Swift's disgust for the masses is evidenced in his novel *Gulliver's Travels* by the noble Houyhnhnm horses and beastly Yahoo men. He thinks of Swift, with a priestly tonsured head, climbing a pole to escape the masses. Stephen thinks of priests all around the city and of the piety and intellectual pretensions of his youth.

Stephen notices he has passed the turnoff for Sara's. Heading toward the Pigeonhouse (Dublin powerplant), Stephen thinks about pigeons: specifically, the Virgin Mary's insistence that her pregnancy was caused by a pigeon (as recorded in Léo Taxil's *La Vie de Jesus*). He thinks of Patrice Egan, the son of Kevin Egan, a "wild goose" (Irish nationalist in exile) whom Stephen knew in Paris. He remembers himself in Paris as a medical student with little money. He remembers arriving once at the post office too late to cash a money order from his mother. Stephen's ambitions for his life in Paris were suddenly halted by a telegram from his father, calling Stephen home to his mother's deathbed: "Mother dying come home." He thinks back to Buck's aunt's insistence that Stephen killed his mother by refusing to pray at her deathbed.

Stephen remembers the sights and sounds of Paris, and of Kevin Egan's conversations about nationalism, strange French customs, and his Irish youth. Stephen walks to the edge of the sea and back, scanning the horizon for the Martello Tower. He again vows not to sleep there tonight with Buck and Haines. He sits on a rock and notices the carcass of a dog. A live dog runs across the beach, back to two people. Stephen imagines the beach scene when the first Danish Vikings invaded Dublin.

The barking dog runs toward Stephen, and Stephen contemplates his fear of the dog. Considering various "Pretenders" to crowns in history, Stephen wonders if he, too, is a pretender. He notices that the two figures with the dog are a man and a woman, cocklepickers. He watches as the dog sniffs at the carcass and is scolded by his master. The dog pisses, then digs in the sand. Stephen remembers his morning riddle about the fox who buried his own grandmother.

Stephen tries to remember the dream he was having last night: a man holding a melon was leading Stephen on a red carpet. Watching the woman cocklepicker, Stephen is reminded of a past sexual encounter in Fumbally's lane. The couple pass Stephen, looking at his hat. Stephen constructs a poem in his head and jots it down on a scrap torn from Deasy's letter. Stephen wonders who the "she" of his poem would be. He longs for affection. Stephen lies back and contemplates his borrowed boots and small feet that once fit into a woman's shoes. He pisses. He thinks again of the drowned man's body. Stephen gets up to leave, picks his nose, then looks over his shoulder to see if anyone has seen. He sees a ship approaching.

There is very little action in Episode Three and only one line of dialogue—"Tatters! Out of that, you mongrel!" Any other dialogue is either imagined or part of flashback episodes. The chapter consists almost entirely of Stephen's thoughts. Joyce's scant use of punctuation makes it somewhat difficult in Episodes One and Two to distinguish between third-person narrative, interior monologue, and dialogue. In Episode Three, the problem becomes not how to distinguish Stephen's interior monologue from all else, but how to follow the twists and turns of that monologue itself. Stephen is an extremely educated young man—his thoughts therefore flit over a host of scholarly texts and several different languages—both direct and oblique references are made to poets, writers, historical figures, and philosophers such as Aristotle (384-322 BC); the Italian mystic Giordano Bruno (1548-1600); the German mystic Jacob Boehme (1575-1624); British philosopher George Berkeley (1685-1753); Andalusian Moorish Arab philosopher, physician and polymath Abu al-Walid Muhammad ibn Ahmad ibn Rushd, better known in the Latin West as Averroës (1126-1198), noted for his commentaries that sought to reconcile Aristotle with Moslem orthodoxy; the Jewish rabbi and talmudic scholar Moses Maimonides (11-35-1204), who tried to reconcile Aristotelian rationalism with the truth of orthodox Judaism; Thomas Aquinas (1225-1274) who, like Averroës and Maimonides, tried to reconcile Aristotlean thought with the revealed truth of Christianity; the Italian Giambattista Vico (1668-1744); the German idealist Georg Wilhelm Friedrich Hegel (1770-1831); the German critic and dramatist Gotthold Ephraim Lessing (1729-1781); English poet and painter William Blake (1757-1827); English essayist, critic, biographer and lexicographer Samuel Johnson (1709-1784); Italian poet Dante Alighieri (1265-1321); English poet, novelist, playwright and critic Algernon Charles Swinburne (1837-1909); Christian presbyter and ascetic Arius (256-336), who was excommunicated for his heresy that God the Father was greater than Jesus Christ the Son who was thus in turn greater than the Holy Sprit—*transubstantiality*—instead of affirming the concept of *consubstantiality*—that the three persons of the Trinity were of the same substance or essence; the comic operas of dramatist W.S. Gilbert (1836-1911) and composer Arthur Sullivan (1842-1900); the Italian mystic Father Joachim of Floris (1145-1202) who prophesized that the world would come to an end in 1260; French watercolorist Madeleine Lemaire (1845-1928); Anglo-Irish satirist and political pamphleteer Jonathan Swift (1667-1745), author of *Gulliver's Travels,* who became Dean of St. Patrick's Cathedral; "fiery" abbot, writer and missionary of the Celtic church, Columbanus (543-615); the English Scholastic, philosopher and theologian William of Occam (1285-1349), noted for the remorseless logic with which he dissected every question—called "Occam's Razor;" English poet John Dryden (1631-1700); Italian Renaissance humanist philosopher and scholar Pico della Mirandola (1463-1494); Shakespeare (1563-1623); French writer M. Léo Taxil, pseudonym of Gabriel Jogand-Pages (1854-1907), known for his *Life of Christ*; Italian opera composer Giuseppe Fortunino Francesco Verdi (1813-1901); Irish poet and founder of the Abbey Theatre William Butler Yeats (1865-1939); French historian of the "Romantic school" Jules Michelet (1798-1874); Welsch poet, critic, and magazine editor Arthur Symons (1865-1945); French poet, critic, and novelist Théophile Gautier (1811-1872); Italian poet, writer and Renaissance humanist Giovanni Boccaccio (1313-1375), known for the *Decamaron*; Irish wit, poet and dramatist Oscar Fingal O'Flahertie Wills Wilde (1854-1900); French sculptor Henri Lemaire (1798-1880; English writer and social critic Charles Dickens (1812-1870), considered by most critics as the greatest novelist of the Victorian era, who created more indelible fictional characters than any other writer, with the possible exception of Shakespeare; Norwegian playwright, poet, and theatre director Henrik Ibsen (1828-1906); English poet Alfred, Lord Tennyson (1809-1892); and numerous references to Biblical passages, to name only a few. Stephen also references contemporary songs, events, personages, and places in Dublin. Episode Three also offers a compendium of the symbols we have seen thus far, as Stephen's mind works in the language of symbols from earlier in the morning. Thus Deasy's shell collection, the sea as mother from Episode One, and drowned male bodies recur in Episode Three and become motifs.

Thus far this morning, we have seen Stephen in his social and professional guises, with smatterings of his private thoughts. The more personal nature of Episode Three allows us to sense an undertone of suffering (expressed through the recurring themes of death, drowning, and decay) in Stephen's thoughts. The Stephen Dedalus from the end of *A Portrait of the Artist as a Young Man* was isolated and full of pride. He had ceased to communicate with those around him, and was cerebrally focused on his artistic coming-of-age and Parisian exile. The Stephen of *Ulysses* is chastened by his untriumphant return to Ireland, and has begun to learn the error of his ways—he must acknowledge and interact with the world around him if he ever wishes to mature as an artist. The beginnings of Stephen's maturation can be seen here in his willingness to be critical of his younger self.

At the beginning of the episode, Stephen briefly considers philosophical solipsism—the idea that the world only exists in our individual perceptions of it. He rehearses the refutation of this theory—knocking his walking-stick against a rock. Despite his practical refutation of solipsism, however, Stephen's attention in the first part of the episode is focused not on his surroundings, but on his thoughts and on his imaginative recreations of his surroundings. As the episode goes on, though, Stephen begins apprehending more and more of his physical surroundings—by the end of the chapter we finally have a sense, for the first time, of the presence of Stephen's body, as he urinates, touches his rotten teeth, picks his nose, and looks over his shoulder. His attentiveness to his own physical presence within his surroundings leads him to produce art. He uses the cocklepicker as concrete inspiration for a poem involving a female figure. Stephen's artistic maturation will not be accomplished today, June 16, 1904, the day Joyce had his first date with Nora Barnacle when she reached into his pants, saying playfully, "What this?" before she brings him to orgasm, after which Joyce kept the white glove she was wearing at his bedside and bought her a new pair of gloves. "Exchange is not thievery," he said. But the direction in which Stephen must continue is laid out for us in Episode Three. Leopold Bloom, appearing finally in Episode Four, also serves as a model of outward attentiveness in opposition to the cerebral Stephen.

Episode 3 is associated with Proteus, the shape-shifting god. Accordingly, the episode is full of transformations of all sorts—reincarnation, reproduction, mystical morphings, and material change. Stephen sees figures and landscapes around him and shape-shifts them in his poetic consciousness—for example, he associates the running dog with a bear, a fawn, a wolf, a calf, a panther, and a vulture. Transformation, in which one element translates into a new context (for example, a soul into a new body), also characterizes the movement of Stephen's thought. His associations and topic-jumps are not always logic-based. They often rely on one word or even the sound of a word to introduce an entirely new thought into his mind. For example, the dog's morphing into a panther brings to mind Haines's dream about a panther, which then causes Stephen to try to remember what he himself had been dreaming about when Haines's moaning woke him.

Thus far in *Ulysses*, we have seen Stephen to be concerned with mothers—for example, his own mother's death, the concept of maternal love, and Eve as the original mother. In Episode Three, we get Stephen's first thoughts about fathers, his own father specifically, from whom Stephen pointedly distances himself here. Kevin Egan, the exiled Irish nationalist, functions as a sort of father figure in Episode Three as well. To the extent that he is paternal, Egan represents the restrictive pull of fidelity to country and to God and to an idealized past—restrictions that Stephen would prefer to avoid. Stephen's actual lack of his mother and his willed lack of a father underlies the movement toward an expected climax in which Stephen might find surrogate parents in Leopold and Molly Bloom.

"Proteus" takes place at about 11:00 A.M. on Sandymount Strand, which is approximately nine miles from Mr. Deasy's school. Stephen wanders along the beach to spend time before he meets Mulligan at The Ship pub at 12:30 P.M. He considers visiting the home of his Aunt Sara and his Uncle Richie Goulding (his mother's relatives), but then he thinks of the ridicule that his father, Simon, has heaped upon Uncle Richie in the past and what Simon might say about today's visit, and he decides not to make the trip. Thus the lengthy description of his visit to the Gouldings concerns only an imagined event.

The first two paragraphs of "Proteus" are especially difficult unless one realizes that Joyce, through a stream-of-consciousness technique, is recording the complexity of Stephen's thoughts as he muses upon the question of what is real, and what is not merely appearance. Stephen is conversant in philosophy as well as in literary theory, and the first two paragraphs mirror his preoccupation with the processes of knowing and being. Although there is probably no exact source that Joyce used for the opening words of the chapter ("Ineluctable modality of the visible"), the subject matter of the following allusions is found in Aristotle's *De Anima*. Joyce may have used an Italian or French translation. Aristotle taught that we are first aware of bodies through their translucence or transparency (diaphane), then through their colors. Dante judged Aristotle to be bright and called him *maestro di color che sanno*, "master of those who know."

The first paragraph questions whether what we see is real; the second, the reality of the audible, as Stephen closes his "eyes to hear." The *nacheinander* refers to objects as they are perceived in time—that is, one after another; the *nebeneinander*, as they are perceived in space—that is, one beside the other. The latter deals with visual appearances; the former, with auditory ones. In *Ulysses*, Stephen must disentangle the reality of his past (in Paris as well as in Dublin) from obfuscating memories; he must discover who he really is, as opposed to the person that others, such as Mulligan, perceive him to be.

The parallels in this chapter with Homer are very general. In the *Odyssey*, Menelaus tells Telemachus how he had to deal with Proteus, the god of the sea who could change forms at will. In order for Menelaus to see Proteus' true form—so he could tell the future—Menelaus had to hold onto Proteus as he went through all his shifts of shape, as if Menelaus were riding a Brahman bull. In *Ulysses*, Proteus is "primal matter" with which Stephen struggles. His thoughts are dense with literary echoes, Latin quotations, and medieval philosophy. It's as if Joyce's 3rd person omniscient narrator had been hijacked, taken over by the character narrated, thus shifting styles and point of view, with lightning transitions mid-sentence, much like Menelaus riding the Brahman bull. So it is not just the shifts in the stream of consciousness technique, but Joyce is mimicking the Protean parallel with the Homeric episode. If the reader feels they're about to lose their literary balance, don't fret: this is the experience Joyce wants you to have. Here, Joyce reveals the changes that are beginning to take place within Stephen, and, through an "interior monologue" technique, Joyce mimes Stephen's shifting thoughts as being like the ever-fluctuating, "protean" nature of reality. The reference to the "winedark" sea pins the chapter to its Greek prototype with its use of a favorite Homeric "epic simile."

Stephen's initial problems in the chapter are philosophical: because all things are bound up in inescapable change ("ineluctable modality"), what is the nature of reality? Does an object exist if no one sees it? Does a sound exist if no creature hears it? Walking along the beach, wearing boots borrowed from Mulligan, Stephen thinks of the many philosophers whom he has read who treated this problem of permanence and change. Aristotle is central among them, as is Bishop George Berkeley (1685-1753), who supposedly denied the objective existence of matter and whom Samuel Johnson purportedly "refuted" by kicking a rock. The capricious nature of reality is epitomized in Stephen's reference to the waves as being the "steeds of Mananaan," the Irish god of the sea, an archetypal jester, who represents change. Once Mananaan resurrected a man from death but put the man's head on backwards, turning his face to the rear—an event which typifies this god of the altered lifestyle.

It is not surprising, then, that in a chapter which concerns the origin and nature of reality, Joyce would insert two women who Stephen pretends are midwives, and these two "midwives" would then make an appearance on the beach, "our mighty mother." These two women are probably from the "liberties," a lower-class section of Dublin, and they are Florence MacCabe, the widow of Patrick MacCabe, and a lady friend. Mrs. MacCabe carries a heavy bag, and Stephen wonders if it contains a "misbirth." Although this gloomy thought is probably occasioned by Stephen's having been reared in a poor environment, it is soon followed by a variety of witty and humorous associations, as Stephen's emotions rapidly fluctuate. Stephen thinks of certain "mystic monks" whose sashes apparently link them together in the present and trace a path back to God. He envisions all navel cords as extending from Eve, and he wonders whether he could place a call on this "telephone connection" back to "Edenville." His reference to "belly without blemish" is descriptive of Eve, who, as a product of Adam's side, did not have a navel; it also suggests the Immaculate Conception of Mary, the Second Eve, who did not have a mortal blemish in her purity.

The antithesis of this birth imagery is seen in the bloated carcass of the dog sniffed by Tatters and in Stephen's vision of the leprous corpse from the sea. The last, like Milton's Edward King (from the poem Stephen was teaching in the previous episode, "Lycidas") was sunk beneath the watery floor, but, unlike King, he undergoes no kind of transformation.

Neither does fatherhood escape unscathed in "Proteus," as Stephen wonders who his real father is: Simon Dedalus, whose act of love was blind, drunken copulation—or God Himself—Whose "coupler's will" Mary and Simon were simply carrying out, and about Whom there is the command of a *lex eternal*— that is, an eternal law. Stephen, looking towards Dublin's electric power station, the Pigeonhouse, thinks of the blasphemous lines from Leo Taxil's *La Vie de Jesus* (1884), in which Joseph asks the pregnant Mary who had put her in this "fichue position," or tough situation; there, Mary answered that it was the pigeon (dove, Holy Ghost, etc.). Thus, Stephen, by implication, shares (symbolically) the nebulous parentage of Christ and of many epic heroes. He is a Telemachus who wonders at this point not where his father is, but who his true father is.

Stephen's psychological dislocation, then, his ability to see only the "signatures of all things," to hear only their sounds, and not to know their essential selves or *noumena*, leads him to think of his many difficulties, past and present. He remembers the lies that he told about his ancestors at school at Clongowes. He recalls that, while others predicted a fine future for him as a religious man (Stephen was ostensibly a saintly lad), he was really thinking about naked women. He also remembers his ostentatious displays of erudition and his wish that should he die, his brother Stanislaus was to send copies of his early, short prose poems, his epiphanies, he called them, to all the major libraries of the world, including the vatican.

The present offers little solace for Stephen. His return from Paris was occasioned by his father's telegram announcing that his mother was dying (the actual telegram had a typing error: "Nother dying, come home"—thus, a "curiosity to show."), and he thinks again of the reason that Buck Mulligan's aunt had forbidden Buck to remain as Stephen's friend: Stephen's refusal to pray at his mother's bedside. He recalls Mulligan's present possession of the key to the Tower. Stephen was afraid of the gypsies' dog, Tatters, and he contrasts himself (again) with Mulligan, who saved a man from drowning. Stephen is supremely sensitive (once again) of his teeth, which he sees as mere shells, an effective image which recalls both Deasy's shell collection in Episode Two, "Nestor" and the beach setting in this chapter. Stephen wonders whether he should use his school pay to see a dentist; then he thinks of the comment made by the anti-Semitic journalist Edouard Adolphe Drumont about Queen Victoria: "Old hag with the yellow teeth."

Stephen's dilemma is defined by Joyce's use of several analogues: (1) Stephen's Uncle Richie sits in bed, calls for whiskey, and "drones bars" from Verdi's *Il Trovatore*; in this opera, the faithful Ferrando is a contrast to the deceiver Mulligan; (2) Jonathan Swift, Stephen feels, was driven mad by the unappreciative rabble and was led to venerate his famous horses in Part IV of *Gulliver's Travels*, the Houyhnhnms; and (3) Kevin Egan, the Fenian whose plans to blow up Parliament, and who rolls cigarettes with gunpowder, led to disaster; even today, he waits as an exiled "wild goose" in Paris for the resurrection of his native Ireland while trying to enlist assistance for his ideas of revolution.

The original of Kevin Egan, one should note, was Joseph Casey, an Irish Nationalist, who, in 1867, was involved in a tragic attempt to free several Fenians from Clerkenwell Prison in London by using gunpowder. Stephen thinks of Egan (whom he met in Paris) several times in the episode, and Egan fits into several major motifs of *Ulysses*. He is an example of a leader who is abandoned and forgotten by the Irish people. His brand of patriotism, the cause for which he tries to enlist Stephen's help, is a temptation that Stephen must avoid if he is to become a detached, objective artist. In Paris, Egan told Stephen tales of disguise and wild escapes, appropriate to this episode ("Proteus"), which deals with illusion. Finally, Kevin Egan fits into the father theme of *Ulysses*, when he tells Stephen to find Patrice, his son, and let him know that Stephen saw him (Kevin Egan). Patrice is Egan's son by his estranged French wife, and one thinks, in contrast, of the less than febrile passion between Bloom and Molly.

It is no wonder, then, that one of the major analogues for Stephen's plight is the *via crucis*. Two shirts are "crucified" on a clothesline, and in the last paragraph of the episode the spars of the three-master ship, the *Rosevean*, recall Christ's death between two thieves, Barabas, known as the Impenitent Thief because he asks Jesus why he couldn't just save himself, and Dismas, known as the Penitent Thief, also known as the Good Thief or the Thief on the Cross, the one who is saved. (See the apocraphal Gospel of Nicodemus).

Change, to Stephen, is a crucifixion, for he must learn to become mature or be drowned by life, to balance the conflicting forces that define him. As a boy, he was full of dreams and secure, despite belonging to a poor family; he accepted his church's teachings and was scholastically successful, confident of his ability to write fine poetry. Now, after living in Paris, a sojourn that accentuated tendencies towards blasphemy and skepticism which had been present in his personality for a long time, he feels lost. Cut off from the old verities, yet unable to slip into Mulligan's glib, atheistic cynicism, Stephen finds himself defenseless and no longer possessed of a belief in the spontaneity of his genius; he must now walk his deeply troubled *Way of the Cross*.

Still, however, the chapter is also about hope, and the prognosis for Stephen is not as bleak as some critics have maintained. It is true that there will be no Tempest-like "seachange" for the drowned and swollen body, but for Stephen there is at least the strong possibility of renewal; and this rebirth is suggested by two crucial actions. In the first, Stephen, realizing the pretentiousness of his earlier literary endeavors, feels the impulse to write a poem, so he tears off part of Deasy's letter and begins to write. In the second, he urinates, an action that in much of *Ulysses* is associated with creativity. In Episode Fourteen, he and Bloom will urinate in the garden, above them "the heaventree of stars hung with humid nightblue fruit." Afterwards Stephen will leave and Bloom will return to the bed where Molly is sleeping, lying beside her head to foot, foot to head, with his face pressed against her plump buttocks.

With Stephen teetering between solvency—both emotional and monetary—and insolvency— hope and despair, sanity and madness, creativity and waste—the first part of *Ulysses* comes to an end. The capital letter S began Stephen's section in "Telemachus"; a capital M, for Molly, will begin Bloom's journey in the next episode, "Calypso."

The fact that the S is used to form part of Mulligan's description ("Stately") and the fact that the M is used to form part of "Mr" Bloom's name refer to the interrelatedness of all things. Stephen, even at the start of his own section, needs the gruff masculinity of Buck, and Bloom and Molly heavily (and perhaps ultimately) depend upon one another.

> *I don't know whether my husband is a genius or not, but he certainly has a dirty mind.*
>
> —Nora Barnacle

James Joyce and Nora Barnacle, seated on a wall in Zurich. Image from the UB James Joyce collection courtesy of the Poetry Collection of the University Libraries, University at Buffalo, the State University of New York.

Episode 3, "Proteus":
Original 1922 Text
with Notes and
Commentary

Sandymount Strand, Howth Head in the distance; Dublin, Ireland

Ineluctable modality of the visible: at least that if no more, thought through my eyes. **Signatures of all things** I am here to read, seaspawn and seawrack, the nearing tide, that rusty boot. Snotgreen, bluesilver, rust: **coloured signs. Limits of the diaphane**. But he adds: in bodies. Then he was aware of them bodies before of them coloured. How? **By knocking his sconce against them**, sure. Go easy. **Bald he was and a millionaire**, *maestro di color che sann*o. Limit of the diaphane in. Why in? Diaphane, adiaphane. If you can put your five fingers through it it is a gate, if not a door. Shut your eyes and see.

Supplemental Notes & Commentary

The mention of "the steps from Leahy's terrace" fixes Stephen's location at the beginning of Episode 3, "Proteus," fairly precisely, and also links him with the location of Bloom in Episode 13, "Nausicaa," where he watches Gerty Macdowell sit provocatively enough to show her underpants whereupon Bloom masturbates watching her. Leahy's Terrace is a road in the southeastern suburb of Sandymount. It runs SW-NE, beginning at Sandymount Road and terminating at the time of the novel at a seawall bordering Sandymount Strand. (Since that time, the land has been reclaimed from the sea, pushing the seacoast further east.)

maestro di color che sanno:
Joyce's language fluency reveals more about this quote from Dante than the fact that it comes from Dante in reference to Aristotle. The context, remember, is perception, immanent reality, the reality of matter (Aristotle) versus the reality of ideal forms which cannot be seen (Plato). How do things appear to our eyes and what is their true essence that vision alone cannot apprehend: semblance vs reality? Surely Joyce loved the ambiguity of the Italian. *Color*, in Italian, can mean "color," but it can also mean "of those." The phrase in Italian can thus be translated as "The master of those who know" or "The master who knows color." Episode 3 begins with Stephen's intense meditation on Aristotle's theories of space and vision. According to Aristotle's natural philosophy and his theory of color, colors have the capacity to cause themselves to be seen. Stephen is pondering whether or not he can see, what he sees with his eyes open, and what he sees with them closed. But more important, he is also pondering whether or not he can be seen at all.

Notes to Bold Phrases in Original Text on Facing Page

Ineluctable modality of the visible: in plain English, the phrase means "the inescapable nature of that which can be seen." Ineluctable is the inability to escape something even with great struggle. You can't escape the visible form of the world no matter how hard you try. The exact phrase is not found literally in Aristotle, but probably comes from a French translation that Joyce would have read while in Paris. This episode with Stephen concerns his contemplation of the inescapability of the material world, and, in particular, that aspect of it which is perceptible through the sense of sight (though Arisitotle, in both his *De Sensu et Sensibili* and *De Anima*, considered perception of the material world through all the senses: sound, taste, touch, smell, temperature, hardness/softness, etc.

Signature of all things: from Jakob Boehme (1575-1624), *Signatura Rerum.* Boehme was a German mystic who maintained that everything that exists is intelligible only through its opposite. Thus the "modality" of visual experience was the signature of its true existence, which was spiritual. One could not know the spiritual nature of God without comprehending His signature as manifested and revealed in the material existence of the world.

coloured signs: The Irish philosopher and Church of Ireland bishop of Cloyne George Berkeley (1685-1753 argued in "An Essay Towards a New Theory of Vision" (1709) that we do not "see" objects as such, rather we see only colored signs and then take these to be objects, though these objects did not exist as material things, but as manifestations of "ideas." This was his primary achievement as a philosopher: the advancement of a theory he called "immaterialism" (later referred to as "subjective idealism" by others). This theory denies the existence of material substance and instead contends that familiar objects like tables and chairs are only ideas in the minds of perceivers and, as a result, cannot exist without being perceived. Berkeley is also known for his critique of abstraction, an important premise in his argument for immaterialism. This foreshadowed his chief philosophical work, *A Treatise Concerning the Principles of Human Knowledge* (1710), which, after its poor reception, he rewrote in dialogue form and published three years later under the title *Three Dialogues between Hylas and Philonous.* He also argued against Isaac Newton's doctrine of absolute space, time and motion in *On Motion*, published 1721. His arguments were a precursor to the views of Mach and Einstein. In 1734, he published *The Analyst*, a critique of the foundations of calculus, which was influential in the development of mathematics.

limits of the diaphane . . . in bodies: transparent

by knocking his sconce against them: if Aristotle knew they were bodies before he formulated a theory of how he perceived them visually, how would he know that they existed? Because he bumped his head against them! This is similar to Samuel Johnson's refutation of the ingenious sophistry Bishop Berkeley used to prove the non-existence of matter, that everything in the universe was but an "idea." As recounted in his *Life of Johnson*, James Boswell reports: "I shall never forget the alacrity with which Johnson answered Berkeley's thesis by striking his foot with mighty force against a large stone, 'till he rebounded from it and fell to the ground, then said, 'I refute it thus!'"

bald he was and a millionaire: We have little biographical information about Aristotle, but medieval embellishments referred to his baldness and his wealth.

maestro di color che sanno: Italian: "master of those who know": from Dante's description of Aristotle in the *Inferno*, Canto IV, line 131 (see note in left column).

adiaphane: non-transparent, opaque.

Stephen closed his eyes to hear his boots crush crackling wrack and shells. You are walking through it howsomever. I am, a stride at a time. A very short space of time through very short times of space. Five, six: the *nacheinander*. Exactly: and that is the ineluctable modality of the audible. Open your eyes. No. Jesus! If I fell over **a cliff that beetles o'er his base**, fell through the nebeneinander ineluctably! I am getting on nicely in the dark. **My ash sword** hangs at my side.

Sandymount Strand, 2021, **Dublin News**

A rustic ash walking stick

nacheinander, one after another in time, *nebeneinder*, next to one another in space. Probably taken from Gotthold Lessing's (1729-81) characterization in *Laocoön* where objects appropriate to poetry in time are contrasted to those appropriate to painting, which exist in space.

A cliff that beetles o'er his base: from *Hamlet*, I:iv.69-78: In Act I, Horatio warms Hamlet of the dangers involved in following the Ghost:

> What if it tempt you toward the flood, my lord
> Or to the dreadful summit of the cliff
> That beetles o'er [juts out over] his base into the sea,
> And there assume some other horrible form
> Which might deprive your sovereignty of reason
> And draw you into maddness? Think of it.
> The very place puts toys of desperation,
> Without more motive, into every brain
> That looks so many fathoms to the sea
> And hears it roar beneath.

My ash sword: An "ashplant" is a walking stick fashioned from an unbarked sapling that has been cut off below the surface of the soil. The main root of many ash saplings takes a horizontal bend for several inches below the surface, before continuing its downward path, and such a sapling supplies a natural handle when the stick is inverted. In Celtic tradition the ash was associated with kingmaking and half the furniture of arms, that is, the handles of spears, were made of it. Stephen may have begun carrying his for protection against dogs, but he thinks of it as also possessing various kinds of magical power. In *James Joyce's Disunited Kingdom and the Irish Dimension* (Gill and Macmillan, 1976), John Garvin devotes a chapter to the ashplant, noting that it is seasoned in a chimney and filled with molten lead. Garvin speculates that Joyce acquired his ashplant during one of his visits to Mullingar and surrounding parts of Westmeath in 1900 and 1901. Stephen's ashplant has a "ferrule," a metal ring or cap placed at the end of the shaft to keep it from splitting or wearing down. In the first episode of *Ulysses*, "Telemachus," the "squealing" of the metal scraping against stone makes Stephen think of a "familiar," the supernatural animal-like spirit which attends a magician. He imagines this little spirit calling "Steeeeeeeeeeeeephen!" as he walks along dragging the stick behind him. At the beginning of "Proteus," Stephen thinks, "My ash sword hangs at my side." Later in the chapter, he lifts his ashplant by its "hilt" as if it were a sword, "lunging with it softly." This playful action anticipates a climactic action in Episode 15, "Circe," when Stephen cries, "Nothung!"—the name of the magic sword in Wagner's *Ring* cycle—and raises it over his head with both hands to smash the chandelier in the brothel. Don Gifford has noted that in the second of the four operas in the cycle, *Die Walküre*, the god Wotan has planted this sword "in the heart of a giant ash tree." Siegfried's father pulls the sword from the tree, and in the final opera of the cycle, *Die Götterdämmerung*, Siegfried unwittingly uses the magic of Nothung to bring about the Twilight of the Gods. The Wagnerian magical subtext empowers Stephen. When he smashes the chandelier he is violently resisting his mother's fiendish call to repent and return to God's grace. The ruin of the lamp makes him think of the "ruin of all space" and time: the destruction of the divinely constituted order which he has been contemplating ever since Episode 2, "Nestor." In "Proteus," Stephen calls his stick "my augur's rod of ash," linking it with another kind of magical power. Just as the shape of the stick has allowed him to think of it as a sword with a hilt, so now it becomes a *lituus*, a staff with one curved end that Roman priests used to consecrate a sector of the sky before reading the appearance of birds for omens. The priests' staffs were elaborately curved, like the crozier of a Christian bishop, but earlier Etruscan brass horns, also called *litui*, had shapes more exactly approximating Stephen's walking stick. Apparently, the name originally referred to a shepherd's crook. Joyce thought of his own ashplant as distinctively Irish, and it has been suggested that Stephen's stick should also be seen as embodying the prophetic power of the ancient Irish *fili*, or bards (The Joyce Project by John Hunt, joyceproject.com).

Tap with it: they do. **My two feet in his boots are at the ends of his legs,** *nebeneinander*. Sounds solid: made by the mallet of Los Demiurgos. **Am I walking into eternity** along Sandymount strand? Crush, crack, crick, crick. **Wild sea money. Dominie Deasy kens them a'.**

Won't you come to Sandymount,
Madeline the mare?

Le sommeil de Manon, oil on canvas, by Madeleine Lemaire (ca. 1906)

Detail of The Last Judgment, relief sculpture by Henri Lemaire on the pediment of the Church of the Madeleine, Paris (1883)

My two feet . . . his legs: Stephen has on shoes and trousers that Mulligan has thrown his way.

made by the mallet of Los Demiurgos; Am I walking into eternity?: from William Blake's *Book of Los* (1795), who created the visible world, thus Los is the creator embodying the creative imagination, contrasted with the "Demiurgos" (from Plato), a subordinate god who created the physical world, and in Gnostic theory and Theosophy, the "architect of the world."

wild sea money: "Shells" is slang for money.

Dominie Deasy kens them a': Scots dialect: *dominie*, "teacher, schoolmaster, pedagogue"; *kens*, "knows,": Also a pun on the Latin *Dominus Deus*, "Lord God." In the previous chapter, Stephen collects his pay from Mr. Garrett Deasy, the pro-British, anti-Semitic Headmaster of the boys' school where Stephen teaches. Deasy is a Protestant from the north of Ireland, condescending to Stephen and not a good listener. His overwrought letter to the editor about foot-and-mouth disease among cattle is the object of mockery among Dublin men for the rest of the day. He lectures Stephen on saving his money.

> "You were not born to be a teacher," he says. "Ireland, they say, has the honour of being the only country which never persecuted the jews. Do you know that? No? And do you know why?" He frowned sternly on the bright air.
> "Why, sir," Stephen asked.
> "Because she never let them in!" A coughball of laughter leaped from his throat dragging after it a rattling chain of phlegm. He turned back quickly, coughing, laughing, his lifted arms waving to the air. "She never let them in," he cried again through his laughter as he stamped on gaitered feet over the gravel of the path. "That's why."

Won't you come to Sandymount / Madeline the mare?: A play on one of two names: Madeleine Lemaire (1845-1928), a French watercolorist whose portraits, floral themes, and illustrations were much in fashion; or Philippe-Joseph Henri Lemaire (1798-1880), a French sculptor who created a well-known relief of the Last Judgment in the tympanum of Paris's Madeleine (the church of St. Mary Magdalene). If the pun holds he could have come to Sandymount and similarly improved the Church of Mary, Star of the Sea, in Leahy's terrace, which Stephen has just passed on his way to Sandymoount strand. Leasy's terrace runs from Sandymount Road to Beach Road (and the shore of Dublin Bay) between Sandymount and Irishtown, one-half mile south of the mouth of the River Liffey. The lines of seemingly nonsensical verse that Stephen imagines as he marches rhythmically ("Crush, crack, crick, crick") along the strand—"Won't you come to Sandymount, / Madeline the mare"—do not appear to quote any preexisting literary text, though perhaps one will eventually be discovered. More likely, Stephen is playing with sounds to make a little poetic composition, as he will do later in this episode when he dwells on the sounds of "mouth to her mouth's kiss." The second line refers punningly to either of these two French visual artists, and the punning continues as Stephen thinks about the lines he has just brought into consciousness. Stephen's lines sound like ballad meter (iambic tetrameter alternating with iambic trimeter), which is commonly used in English and Irish popular songs and poems. Regardless of whether Stephen is recalling a popular song in the first line or making one up, his imagination is clearly at work in the second line. Madeleine Lemaire was sometimes called The Empress of the Roses, and she was a fixture of the artistic salons in Paris and was one of Marcel Proust's high-society intimates. If Madeline the mare is Madeleine Lemaire, then Stephen—who perhaps encountered her works or her reputation in Paris—may be wishing that this elegant French artiste would come to Dublin and lend some class to the local literary scene. Of course, it is entirely possible that Stephen is thinking of both Lemaires; nor do the verbal acrobatics stop there. His linguistic imagination is still romping as he contemplates the "Rhythm" of the lines, fancying that his "catalectic tetrameter of iambs" is "marching."

Rhythm begins, you see. I hear. **Acatalectic** tetrameter of iambs marching. **No, agallop:** *deline the mare*.

Open your eyes now. I will. One moment. Has all vanished since? If I open and am for ever in the black adiaphane. *Basta!* I will see if I can see.

See now. There all the time without you: and ever shall be, world without end.

They came down the steps from Leahy's terrace prudently, **Frauenzimmer**: and down the shelving shore flabbily, their splayed feet sinking in the silted sand. Like me, **like Algy, coming down to our mighty mother**. Number one swung **lourdily** her midwife's bag, the other's **gamp** poked in the beach. From **the liberties**, out for the day. Mrs Florence MacCabe, relict of the late Patk MacCabe, deeply lamented, of Bride Street. One of her sisterhood lugged me squealing into life. Creation from nothing. What has she in the bag? A misbirth with a trailing navelcord, hushed in ruddy wool. The cords of all link back, strandentwining cable of all flesh. That is why mystic monks. **Will you be as gods?** Gaze in your **omphalos**. Hello! Kinch here. Put me on to Edenville. Aleph, alpha: nought, nought, one.

Algernon Charles Swinburne (5 April 1837–10 April 1909) was an English poet, playwright, novelist, and critic. He wrote several novels and collections of poetry such as *Poems and Ballads*, and contributed to the famous Eleventh Edition of the *Encyclopædia Britannica.*

Swinburne wrote about many taboo topics, such as lesbianism, cannibalism, sado-masochism, and anti-theism. His poems have many common motifs, such as the ocean, time, and death. Several historical people are featured in his poems, such as Sappho ("Sapphics"), Anactoria ("Anactoria"), and Catullus ("To Catullus").

Pre-Raphaelites, including Dante Gabriel Rossetti. He also met William Morris. After leaving college, he lived in London and started an active writing career, where Rossetti was delighted with his "little Northumbrian friend," probably a reference to Swinburne's diminutive height—he was just five-foot-four.

Algernon Charles Swinburne, 1862, by Dante Gabriel Rossetti

Swinburne was an alcoholic and algolagniac and highly excitable. He liked to be flogged. His health suffered, and in 1879 at the age of 42, he was taken into care by his friend, Theodore Watts-Dunton, who looked after him for the rest of his life at The Pines, 11 Putney Hill, Putney. Watts-Dunton took him to the lost town of Dunwich, on the Suffolk coast, on several occasions in the 1870s.

In Watts-Dunton's care Swinburne lost his youthful rebelliousness and developed into a figure of social respectability. It was said of Watts-Dunton that he saved the man and killed the poet. Swinburne died at the Pines on 10 April 1909, at the age of 72, and was buried at St. Boniface Church, Bonchurch on the Isle of Wight. (Wikipedia)

No, agallop: *deline the mare:* Lemaire is now fully a mare, galloping along the shore of the mare (Latin for sea).

Acatalectic: "Catalectic": poetic metrics—lacking either a syllable in the last foot, or an initial unstressed syllable. "Acatalectic", is not catalectic, so the line is complete in its syllables. If Stephen is right and these lines are iambic (only the first would be tetrameter), then they would be "catalectic"—missing the first unstressed syllable. The first two editions had it as "A catalectic," but Joyce later made some amendations and there's still some debate on this point. In an unpublished letter, Joyce included a postscript: "divide better A catalectic." One would assume this was his final word on the matter.

Frauenzimmer: German originally for a "lady of fashion" but then used as a sign of contempt for a "nitwit, drab, sloven, wench."

Like Algy . . . our mighty mother: reference to Algernon Charles Swinburne (1837-1909), who wrote in his poem "The Triumph of Time" (1866), "I will go back to the great sweet mother, / Mother and lover of men, the sea." Yeats considered Swinburne the "King of the Cats," or the grand old man of the preceding century's avant-garde. In Episode 1, "Telemachus," Buck Mulligan looks out over Dublin Bay and says: "Isn't the sea what Algy calls it : a great sweet mother? The snotgreen sea. The scrotumtightening sea."

lourdily: heavily, after the French *lourd,* "heavy."

gamp: a large, bulky umbrella, after Mrs. Sairey Gamp in Dickens's *Martin Chuzzlewit* (1843). Mrs Gamp not only carries a large, badly wrapped umbrella, she is also nurse and midwife in the novel.

the liberties: reference to the Liberty Boys (gangs of immigrant Protestant workers) who caused much civic disorder. In 1904, the "liberties" was a run-down section, largely slum, in central Dublin south of the Liffey. The area originally got it's name because it was composed of large estates, two medieval cathedrals, Christ Church and Saint Patrick's—properties which were exempt from taxation.

Will you be as Gods?: Satan says to Eve (Genesis, 3:5) "For God doth know that in the day ye eat thereof, then your eyes shall be opened, and ye shall be as gods, knowing good and evil."

omphalos: Greek: "naval," "center point." In the *Odyssey,* one of Homer's epithets for Ogygia, Calypso's island where Odysseus is stalled at the beginning of the epic, is "naval of the sea." The Oracle at Delphi was marked by a conically-shaped stone, also an omphalos ("the naval of the earth") and the center of prophecy in ancient Greece. Some late-nineteenth century Theosophists contemplated the omphalos variously as the place of the "astral soul of man," the center of self-consciousness and the source of poetic and prophetic inspiration.

At this point in the episode, Joyce has confounded the reader with dramatic shifts in point-of-view, oscillations from interior monologue to the scattered images, bodily sensations, and cerebral associations that pop in and out of Stephen's consciousness. Added to this are Joyce's use of malapropisms, spoonerisms, and word puns ("whiteheaped corn", "strandentwining cable of all flesh"), those verbal emblems of coincidence that wreak havoc with space and time. Protean disarrangment. Memory itself an escape hatch freeing reader and protagonist from the geography of space and events in time, the warp and woof of space-time itself fabling into literary art. As Bloom says: "Think you're escaping and run into yourself." Proteus is exemplified by the changeability of the mind, the endless metamorphosis of our ways of thinking. It's okay, dear reader, if you feel disoriented—Stephen constantly changes his focus and his attitude from intellectual playfulness to bitter despair; even his inner monologue adopts different styles, syntactical rhythms, and flexible prosody.

Spouse and helpmate of **Adam Kadmon:_Heva, naked Eve. She had no navel**. Gaze. <u>Belly without blemish</u>, bulging big, a buckler of taut vellum, no, <u>whiteheaped corn</u>, orient and immortal, standing from everlasting to everlasting. **Womb of sin**.

Wombed in sin darkness I was too, **made not begotten**. By them, the man with my voice and my eyes and a ghostwoman with ashes on her breath. They clasped and sundered, did **the coupler's will. From before the ages He willed me and now may not will me away or ever. A** *lex eterna_*stays about Him. Is that then **the divine substance wherein Father and Son are consubstantial**?

James Joyce

Adam Kadmon: Theosophical name for the first Adam, a prelapsarian human: complete, androgynous, unfallen. From Madame Blavatsky's *Isis Unveiled* (1886): "Starting as a pure and perfect spiritual being, the Adam of the second chapter of *Genesis* is not satisfied with the position allotted to him by the Demiurgos. Adam the second, man of dust, strives in his pride to become Creator in his turn."

Heva, naked . . . no navel: Cheva, Hebrew: "Life"; an early version of Eve's name. Cabalistic tradition according to Madame Blavatsky's Theosophist *Isis Unveiled*, held that Even had no navel because he was not born of woman.

Belly without blemish: Song of Solomon 4:7: Thou art all fair, my love; there is no spot in thee." (Christ in praise of his spouse, the Church).

whiteheaped corn: "Thy navel is like a round goblet, which wanteth not liquor: thy belly is like an heap of wheat set about with lilies" (Song of Solomon, 7:2).

Womb of sin: Eve's belly, because through her (and through Adam) sin came into the world.

made not begotten: The Nicene Creed (325 AD) maintains that Jesus, unlike all otehr men, was "begotten, but not made, of one essence consubstantial with the Father." The creed froms part of the ordinary Mass on all Sundays and on more important feast days.

the coupler's will: God is the "coupler" who joins man and woman together in the sacrement of marriage. His "will," according to Catholic doctrine, is that humankind should "increase and multiply" (Genesis 1:28) by having as many children as possible.

From before the ages He . . . A *lex eterna* stays about Him: Lex eterna, Latin: "eternal law." In the *Summa Theologica*, Thomas Acquinas discusses the implication of the fact that God's law is eternal. Thing which have not come about (in human time) exist in Him already, have always existed and will always exist. From the human point of view, man, who exists in time, may assume that God summon future things, but he doesn't, they are already existing in time. Acquinas says: "The ruling idea of things which exists in God as the effective sovereign of them all has the nature of law. Then since God's mind does not conceive in time, but has an eternal concept . . . it follows that this law should be called eternal. Hence 1. While not as yet existing in themselves things nevertheless exist in God in so far as they are foreseen and preordained by Him; so St. Paul speaks of God *summoning things that are not yet in existence as if they already were*. Thus the eternal concept of divine law bears the character of a law that is eternal as being God's ordination for the governance of things he foreknows."

divine substance . . . consubstantial: Stephen seems to suggest that Father and Son are consubstantial only in their sharing an eternal law. Consubstantial (Latin: *consubstantialis*) is an adjective used in Latin Christian christology, coined by Tertullian in *Against Hermogenes*, used to translate the Greek term *homoousios*. "Consubstantial" describes the relationship among the Divine persons of the Christian Trinity and connotes that God the Father, God the Son, and God the Holy Ghost are "of one substance" in that the Son is "begotten" "before all ages" or "eternally" of the Father's own being, from which the Spirit also eternally "proceeds." In Latin languages it is the term for *homoousism*. The three persons of the Trinity are equal, one and the same, of the same substance, one and separate. Holy Spirit is not less than Christ, and Christ is not less than the Father.

Where is poor dear **Arius to try conclusions? Warring his life long upon the contransmagnificandjewbangtantiality. Illstarred heresiarch' in a Greek watercloset he breathed his last:** euthanasia. With beaded mitre and with crozier, stalled upon his throne, widower of a widowed see, with upstiffed omophorion, with clotted hinderparts.

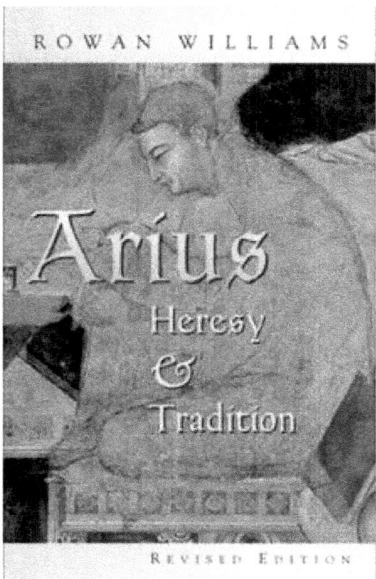

Arius' Theology Fail—paraphrased

Arius (c. 250-336 A.D.)

ROWAN WILLIAMS

Arius
Heresy & Tradition

REVISED EDITION

Arius to try conclusions . . . . breathed his last: Arius is notable primarily because of his role in the Arian controversy, a great fourth-century theological conflict centered on the nature of the Godhead in Christianity that rocked the Christian world and led to the calling of the first ecumenical council of the Church convened by Emperor Constantine the Great in 325. Arius (256–336) was a Christian presbyter who emphasized the Father's divinity over the Son, and his opposition to what would become the dominant Christology, Homoousian Christology, made him a primary topic of the First Council of Nicaea. His heresy was to maintain that the Father and the Son were not of the same, but merely "similar", substance (the Son being the Father's first creation and therefore inferior to Him). Arius died of "hemorhage of the bowels" (intestinal cancer?) on the eve of what would have been a great triumph for him and his followers. Arius was to be no longer an excommunicant as the Emperor ordered the Bishop of Constantinople to administer Holy Communion. His death in a "public toilet" was described by Socrates Scholasticus (a bitter enemy to Arius) as follows:

> "It was then Saturday, and Arius was expecting to assemble with the church on the day following: but divine retribution overtook his daring criminalities. For going out of the imperial palace, attended by a crowd of Eusebian partisans like guards, he paraded proudly through the midst of the city, attracting the notice of all the people. As he approached the place called Constantine's Forum, where the column of Porphyry is erected, a terror arising from the remorse of conscience seized Arius, and with the terror a violent relaxation of the bowels: he therefore enquired whether there was a convenient place near, and being directed to the back of Constantine's Forum, he hastened thither. Soon after a faintness came over him, and together with the evacuations his bowels protruded, followed by a copious hemorrhage, and the descent of the smaller intestines: moreover portions of his spleen and liver were brought off in the effusion of blood, so that he almost immediately died. The scene of this catastrophe still is shown at Constantinople, as I have said, behind the shambles in the colonnade: and by persons going by pointing the finger at the place, there is a perpetual remembrance preserved of this extraordinary kind of death."
>
> Arian' Christian churches persisted throughout Europe, the Middle East, and North Africa and also in various Germanic kingdoms, until suppressed by military conquest or voluntary royal conversion between the fifth and seventh centuries.

to try conclusions: Hamlet, in the bedroom scene (III.iv.194-96), mocks his mother and suggests that she will, against all better judgment, betray him to his uncle Claudius, "and like the famous ape, / To try conclusions, in the basket creep / And break your own neck down" (Gifford and Seidman, *Ulysses Annotated*).

contransmagnificandjewbangtantiality: includes *consubstantiality* and *transsub*stantiality, which Arius affirmed. "Magnific" suggest *Magnificat* (The Blessed Virgin Mary's song of thanksgiving for her role in the Word-made-flesh, Luke 1:46-55) plus *magnificent* and *magnify*. "Jew" is a reminder that the Son was born of a Jew and rejected by the Jews. "Bang" suggests both the controversial origin of Christianity and the sustained controversy over Arianism (The Joyce Project by John Hunt, joyceproject.com).

Airs romped round him, **nipping and eager airs**. They are coming, waves. The whitemaned seahorses, champing, brightwindbridled, **the steeds of Mananaan**.

I mustn't forget his letter for the press. And after? **The Ship**, half twelve. By the way go easy with that money like a good young imbecile. Yes, I must.

His pace slackened. Here. Am I going to **aunt Sara's** or not? My consubstantial father's voice. Did you see anything of your artist brother Stephen lately? No? Sure he's not down in Strasburg terrace with his aunt Sally? **Couldn't he fly a bit higher than that**, eh? And and and and tell us, Stephen, how is uncle Si? O, weeping God, the things I married into! De boys up in de hayloft. The drunken little costdrawer and his brother, the cornet player. **Highly respectable gondoliers**! And **skeweyed Walter sirring his father**, no less! Sir. Yes, sir. No, sir. **Jesus wept**: and no wonder, by Christ!

I pull the wheezy bell of their shuttered cottage: and wait. They take me for a dun, peer out from a **coign of vantage**.

—It's Stephen, sir.

—Let him in. Let Stephen in.

A bolt drawn back and Walter welcomes me.

—We thought you were someone else.

In his broad bed nuncle Richie, pillowed and blanketed, extends over the hillock of his knees a sturdy forearm. Cleanchested. He has washed the upper moiety.

—Morrow, nephew.

He lays aside the lapboard whereon he drafts his bills of costs for the eyes of **master Goff** and master **Shapland Tandy**, filing consents and common searches and a writ of *Duces Tecum*. A bogoak frame over his bald head: **Wilde's Requiescat**. The drone of his misleading whistle brings Walter back.

Laurence Sterne (1713–1768) was an English novelist and an Anglican clergyman. In *The Life and Opinions of Tristram Shandy, Gentleman*, Sterne manipulates narrative time and voice, parodies accepted narrative form, and includes a healthy dose of "bawdy" humor. The novel itself is difficult to describe. The story starts with the narration, by Tristram, of his own conception. It proceeds by fits and starts, but mostly by what Sterne calls "progressive digressions" so that we do not reach Tristram's birth before the third volume. The novel is rich in characters and humor, and ends after nine volumes, published over a decade, but without anything that might be considered a traditional conclusion. Sterne inserts sermons, essays and legal documents into the pages of his novel; and he explores the limits of typography and print design by including marbled pages and, most famously, an entirely black page within the narrative. Many of the innovations that Sterne introduced, adaptations in form that should be understood as an exploration of what constitutes the novel, were highly influential to Modernist writers like James Joyce and Virginia Woolf, and more contemporary writers such as Thomas Pynchon and David Foster Wallace. Italo Calvino referred to *Tristram Shandy* as the "undoubted progenitor of all avant-garde novels of our century." The Russian Formalist writer Viktor Shklovsky regarded it as the archetypal, quintessential novel, of which all other novels are mere subsets: "*Tristram Shandy* is the most typical novel of world literature." (Wikipedia)

nipping and eager airs: Horatio to Hamlet as they watch on the battlements for the appearance of the Ghost (I:iv.2).

Mananaan MacLir (Gaelic: Manannán Mac Lir) is the Irish God of the Sea, the waves are the manes of his horses. He shares Proteus's ability to change form.

his letter for the press: Stephen promised Deasy he'd take the letter he wrote about cattle with foot and mouth disease. At the end of this episode, Stephen, looking for something to write his poem on, tears a piece from the letter.

The Ship: a hotel and tavern at 5 Abbey Street Lower, in the northeast quadrant of Dublin not far from the Liffey. Stephen had agreed to meet Buck Mulligan for drinks there at 12:30.

Aunt Sara's: Sara Goulding, the wife of Richie Goulding, Stephen's mother's brother. They are modeled on Joyce's aunt and uncle, Mr. and Mrs. William Murray. Richie is a law clerk, who has been less able to work recently because of a bad back—a fact that makes him an object of ridicule for Stephen's father, Simon Dedalus. Richie and Sara's son, Walter, is "skeweyed" and has a stutter.

Couldn't he fly a bit higher than that? That is, without the risk of becoming an Icarus.

costdrawer: a cost accountant, similar to a certified public accountant.

Highly respectful gondoliers: Like characters in the comic opera by Gilbert and Sullivan, *The Gondoliers* (1889), in which the phrase occurs several times in a song sung by Don Alhambra in Act I: "I stole the Prince, and brought him here, / And left him gaily prattling / With a highly respectful gondolier, / Who promised the Royal babe to rear / And teach him the trade of timoneer / With his own beloved bratling." The bratling and the Prince look so much alike that not even the respectful gondolier could them apart when he was alive; and he has died of gout and drink. Who is to distinguish between the prince and the pauper?

Jesus wept: The shortest verse in the Bible (John 11:35), as Jesus approaches the tomb of Lazarus.

coign of vantage: As Duncan and his courtiers approach Macbeth's castle they compliment its beauties, and Banquo remarks of the martelet (a kind of swallow): "No jutty, frieze, / Buttress, nor coign of vantage but this bird / Hath made his pendant bed and procreant cradle. Where they most breed and haunt, I have observed / The air is delicate."

master Shapland Tandy: Combines Irish revolutionary and reformer James Napper Tandy (1740-1803) who was a sympathizer with the French Revolution and a key figure in the attempt to secure French aid and support in the Irish struggle for independence, and the eccentric hero from *Tristram Shandy* (1760-67), Laurence Stern's strange, endlessly complex masterpiece. No one description will fit this novel. It is a fiction about fiction-writing in which the invented world is as much infused with wit and genius as the theme of inventing it. It is a joyful celebration of the infinite possibilities of the art of fiction, and a wry demonstration of its limitations. Published in nine volumes over the course of seven years, the novel anticipated modern avant-garde literature (and *Ulysses*) by toying with the limitations of language, events occurring out of chronological order, anecdotes left unfinished, and sometimes whole pages filed with asterisks or dashes or left entirely blank.

Duces Tecum: Latin: "Bring with you"; legal writ demanding that person to appear in court with specific evidence

Wilde's *Requiescat*: Latin "Let her rest"; Wilde's poem (1881) on the death of his sister.

—Yes, sir?

—Malt for Richie and Stephen, tell mother. Where is she?

—Bathing Crissie, sir.

Papa's little bedpal. Lump of love.

—No, uncle Richie . . . .

—Call me Richie. Damn your **lithia water**. It lowers. Whusky!

—Uncle Richie, really . . . .

—Sit down or by the law Harry I'll knock you down.

Walter squints vainly for a chair.

—He has nothing to sit down on, sir.

—He has nowhere to put it, you mug. Bring in our chippendale chair. Would you like a bite of something? None of your damned lawdeedaw airs here. The rich of a rasher fried with a herring? Sure? So much the better. We have nothing in the house but backache pills.

All'erta!

He drones bars of Ferrando's *aria di sortita*. The grandest number, Stephen, in the whole opera. Listen.

His tuneful whistle sounds again, finely shaded, with rushes of the air, his fists bigdrumming on his padded knees.

This wind is sweeter.

Houses of decay, mine, his and all. You told the **Clongowes** gentry you had an uncle a judge and an uncle a general in the army. Come out of them, Stephen. Beauty is not there. Nor in the **stagnant bay of Marsh's library** where you read the fading prophecies of **Joachim Abbas**.

Joachim of Fiore "studying" at his desk.

All saints blessed Joachim of Fiore.

Lithia: bottled spring water.

aria di sortita: Italian "On guard!"; opening words of the opening aria (Ferrando's *aria di sortita*: "entrance aria") in Giuseppe Verdi's (1813-1901) opera *Il Trovatore* (1852)

in the stagnant bay of Marsh's library: St. Sepulchre Library in the close of St. Patrick's Cathedral, founded in 1707 by Narcissus Marsh, archbishop of Dublin, is the oldest public library in Ireland.

Stagnant bay: the interior was still as it was when first constructed, with wire-cage alcoves where readers could be locked while they read particularly valuable books, some still secured by chains to rods. Most guidebooks regard it as "charming" and "quaintly picturesque."

Clongowes: (*cluain*: Irish for "meadow" and *gobha* for "blacksmith") noted for its strong pedigree in rugby, Clongowes Wood College is an independent secondary boarding school for boys from Ireland and other parts of the world which was featured prominently in Joyce's semi-autobiographical novel *A Portrait of the Artist as a Young Man*. Chapter 5, 25 March, Morning: "A long curving gallery. From the floor ascend pillars of dark vapours. It is peopled by the images of fabulous kings, set in stone. Their hands are folded upon their knees in token of weariness and their eyes are darkened for the errors of men go up before them for ever as dark vapours."

Joachim Abbas: Father Joachim of Floris (1145-1202). Italian mystic theologian whose apocalyptic visions divided history into three ages corresponding to the three members of the Trinity: that of the Father, from the creation to the birth of Christ; that of the Son, from the birth of Christ to 1260; and that of the Holy Spirit, from 1260 onward, when a new gospel, the "*evangelium aeternum,*" the everlasting gospel, that would supersede the Old and New Testaments. Thus, they would soon be in the third stage and the end of the world was coming. In the course of the 13th century, many eschatologies appeared that derived from the Book of Revelation and the Sibylline Oracles. Joachim's messianic prophecy became the most influential system known to Europe until the appearance of Marxism. He spent many years brooding over the Scriptures as a Calabrian abbot and hermit, and received an inspiration which seemed to reveal in them a concealed meaning of unique predictive value. That the Scriptures possessed concealed meanings was far from being new, but Joachim's allegorical and typological interpretation was applied, not to the usual moral purposes, but as a means of understanding and forecasting the development of history. There is a certain irony in the fact that no less than three popes urged him to write down his divine revelations, even though they were unorthodox, but in the whole Middle Ages there was scarcely another intellectual who did so much to shake not only the structure of orthodox medieval theology but also the assumptions which must underlie any conceivable Christian faith. In effect, his theory implied that in the third stage, the stage of the Holy Spirit, the Church would be unnecessary, which, of course, was considered heretical. The Fourth Council of the Lateran, in 1215, condemned some of his ideas about the nature of the Trinity. In 1263, the archbishop Fiorenzo enhanced the condemnation of his writings and those of his follower Gerardo of Borgo San Donnino, joining a commission in the Synod of Arles, in which Joachim's theories were declared heretical. The accusation was of having an unorthodox view of the Holy Trinity. His views also inspired several subsequent movements: the Amalricians, the Dulcinians and the Brethren of the Free Spirit. All of these were eventually declared heretical by the Catholic Church. Of importance is the fact that Joachim himself was never condemned as a heretic by the Church; rather, the ideas and movement surrounding him were condemned. Joachim the man was held in high regard during his lifetime. Apparently spurred by Yeats's short story "The Tables of the Law" (1897), Joyce visited Marsh's Library on October 22nd and 23rd to consult a volume in Italian and Latin that includes a text purportedly by Joachim as well as biographical notes of uncertain reliability (The Joyce Project by John Hunt, joyceproject.com).

For whom? The **hundredheaded rabble of the cathedral close. A hater of his kind ran from them to the wood of madness**, his mane foaming in the moon, his eyeballs stars. **Houyhnhnm, horsenostrilled**. The oval equine faces, Temple, Buck Mulligan, **Foxy Campbell, Lanternjaws**. Abbas father,—**furious dean**, what offence laid fire to their brains? Paff!

Jonathan Swift by Charles Jervas (detail)

Anglo-Irish poet, satirist, essayist, and political pamphleteer **Jonathan Swift** was born in Dublin, Ireland. He spent much of his early adult life in England before returning to Dublin to serve as Dean of St. Patrick's Cathedral for the last 30 years of his life. It was this later stage when he would write most of his greatest works. Best known as the author of *A Modest Proposal* (1729), *Gulliver's Travels* (1726), and *A Tale of a Tub* (1704), Swift is widely acknowledged as the greatest prose satirist in English literature. Swift's father died months before Jonathan was born, and his mother returned to England shortly after giving birth, leaving Jonathan in the care of his uncle in Dublin. Swift's extended family had several interesting literary connections: his grandmother, Elizabeth (Dryden) Swift, was the niece of Sir Erasmus Dryden, grandfather of the poet John Dryden. The same grandmother's aunt, Katherine (Throckmorton) Dryden, was a first cousin of Elizabeth, wife of Sir Walter Raleigh. His great-great grandmother, Margaret (Godwin) Swift, was the sister of Francis Godwin, author of *The Man in the Moone*, which influenced parts of Swift's *Gulliver's Travels*. His uncle, Thomas Swift, married a daughter of the poet and playwright Sir William Davenant, a godson of William Shakespeare. Swift's uncle served as Jonathan's benefactor, sending him to Trinity College Dublin, where he earned his BA and befriended writer William Congreve. The Glorious Revolution of 1688 forced Jonathan to move to England, where he would work as a secretary to a diplomat. He would earn an MA from Hart Hall, Oxford, in 1692, and eventually a Doctor in Divinity degree from Trinity College in 1702. Swift's poetry has a relationship either by interconnections with, or by reactions against, the poetry of his contemporaries and predecessors. He was probably influenced, in particular, by the Restoration writers John Wilmot, Earl of Rochester and Samuel Butler (who shared Swift's penchant for octosyllabic verse). He may have picked up pointers from the Renaissance poets John Donne and Sir Philip Sidney. Beside these minor borrowings of his contemporaries, his debts are almost negligible. In the Augustan Age, an era which did not necessarily value originality above other virtues, his poetic contribution was strikingly original. In reading Swift's poems, one is first impressed with their apparent spareness of allusion and poetic device. Anyone can tell that a particular poem is powerful or tender or vital or fierce, but literary criticism seems inadequate to explain why. A few recent critics have carefully studied his use of allusion and image, but with only partial success. It still seems justified to conclude that

Swift continued on 76

The hundredheaded rabble of the cathedral close: In 1901, Joyce wrote an essay for a college magazine, *St. Stephen's*, but it was eventually rejected because in Joyce's scathing indictment of the Irish Literary Theate, he had referenced D'Annunzio's *Il Fuoco*, then on the Catholic Index of banned books. Joyce undertook the printing and distribution of the essay himself. Eighty-five copies of "The Day of the Rabblement" was printed by Gerrard Brothers, a stationary shop across from the college. Its opening sentence quoted what Joyce called "a radical principle of artistic economy" from the Italian philosopher-mystic Giordano Bruno (1548-1600) of Nola whom Joyce regarded as the "father of what is called modern philosophy." Bruno postulated an *anima del mondo* ("soul of the world"), which was an indwelling presence in the light of which form and matter, being and the capacity to be, are not separable as Aristotle thought them, but one, a unity. Madame Blavatsky's theosophist writings noted that this soul of the world was the "divine essence which pervades, permeates, animates and informs all things from the smallest atom of matter to man and God." The sentence from Bruno that Joyce opened his essay with was: "No man, said the Nolan, can be a lover of the true or the good unless he abhors the multitude; and the artist, though he may employ the crowd, is very careful to isolate himself." At the beginning of the century St. Patrick's close—an area immediately around a cathedral, sometimes extending for a hundred metres or more from the main cathedral building, usually including buildings housing diocesan offices, schools, free-standing chapels associated with the cathedral, and the palace of the bishop and other clergy houses associated with the cathedral—was at the heart of a teeming slum.

A hater of his kind ran from them to the wood of madness: Jonathan Swift (1667-1744) was widely regarded as a misanthrope, his hatred of mankind a product of Ménière's disease, which increased deafness, and eventually causing him to sink into madness. Swift claimed that he loved individuals but hated mankind in general. By the time he was seventy-two, cut off from the world by deafness, he suffered the final indignity of a rapidly advancing senility.

Houyhnhnms, horsenostrilled: The Houyhnhnms were the utterly rational horses met by the eponymous hero of *Gulliver's Travels* (1726). Brutish in form but entirely rational in behavior, they are contrasted with the Yahoos, their utter opposites. The **"furious dean"** is obviously Swift.

Foxy Campbell, Lanternjaws: nicknames for Father Campbell, one of the teachers at Belvedere College when Joyce (and Stephen) were students there.

Exile, Censorship, and the Banning of Books

Joyce's artistic struggles involved censorship, exile, and the banning of *Ulysses* in England and the United States. His first experience with the censors occurred when he was 17 when the president of the University College, Dublin, referred to as "the Censor," tried to suppress Joyce's essay "Drama and Life," because Joyce had claimed the poet was emancipated from moral laws. This conflict affected the content of *Stephen Hero*, the book that eventually became *Portrait of the Artist as a Young Man*. This and other conflicts with "the Censor" led to Joyce's self-exile from Ireland shortly after Grant Richards refused to publish *Dubliners*. "The Dead," the final story in that collection, was Joyce's "first song of exile," as Richard Ellman put it in his biography of Joyce.

Joyce's second experience with the censors happened two years after he wrote a paper titled "Drama and Life, in which he attacked Dublin's Irish Literary Theatre for producing mediocre, moralistic, plays. The University College magazine, *St. Stephen's*, refused to publish "The Day of the Rabblement," because of "the Censor," wrote Joyce. The next work to fall prey to the Censor was "The Holy Office," a broadside in which Joyce attacked his Irish contemporaries for their hypocritical prudery, and declared that he would be "the holy office," exposing what they feared to discuss. The broadside was submitted and, for the second time, *St. Stephen's* refused to publish it. A few years later, when he submittted his essay "A Portrait of the Artist," it was rejected because

Exile continued on 77

Descende, calve, ut ne amplius decalveris. A garland of grey hair on **his comminated head** see him me clambering down to the footpace (*descende*), clutching a monstrance, basiliskeyed. Get down, baldpoll! A choir gives back menace and echo, assisting about the **altar's horns**, the snorted Latin of **jackpriests** moving burly in their albs, tonsured and oiled and gelded, fat with **the fat of kidneys of wheat**.

(Swift continued from 74)

Swift's straightforward poetic style seldom calls for close analysis, his allusions seldom bring a whole literary past back to life, and his images are not very interesting in themselves. In general, Swift's verses read faster than Dryden's or Pope's, with much less ornamentation and masked wit. He apparently intends to sweep the reader along by the logic of the argument to the several conclusions he puts forth. He seems to expect that the reader will appreciate the implications of the argument as a whole, after one full and rapid reading. For Swift's readers, the couplet will not revolve slowly upon itself, exhibiting intricate patterns and fixing complex relationships between fictive worlds and contemporary life. The poems are not always as spare in reality as Swift would have his readers believe, but he seems deliberately to induce in them an unwillingness to look closely at the poems for evidence of technical expertise. He does this in part by working rather obviously against some poetic conventions, in part by saying openly that he rejects poetic cant, and in part by presenting himself—in many of his poems—as a perfectly straightforward man, incapable of a poet's deviousness. By these strategies, he directs attention away from his handling of imagery and meter, even in those instances where he has been technically ingenious. For the most part, however, the impression of spareness is quite correct; and if judged by the sole criterion of technical density, then he would have to be judged an insignificant poet. But technical density is a poetic virtue only as it simulates and accompanies subtlety of thought. One could argue that Swift's poems create a density of another kind: that "The Day of Judgement," for example, initiates a subtle process of thought that takes place after, rather than during, the reading of the poem, at a time when the mind is more or less detached from the printed page. One could argue as well that Swift makes up in power what he lacks in density: that the strength of the impression created by his directness gives an impetus to prolonged meditation of a very high quality. On these grounds, valuing Swift for what he really is and does, one must judge him a major figure in poetry as well as prose. Swift suffered a stroke in 1742, leaving him unable to speak. He died three years later, and was buried at St. Patrick's Cathedral, Dublin ("Jonathan Swift," poetryfoundation. org).

Descende, calve, ut ne amplius decalveris. Latin: "Come down, bald one, lest you be made balder."
Allusion to 2 Kings, 2:23 (children's taunt to Elisha: "Go up, thou bald head; go up, thou bald
head") which Joyce spuriously attriibuted to a Joachim Abbas text in Marsh's Library.

his comminated head: "threatened," as with anathama.

the altar's horns: associated with sacrifice. "And thou shalt take of the blood of the bullock, and
put it upon the horns of the altar with thy finger, and pour all the blood beside the bottom of the
altar" (Exodus 29:12). "God is the Lord, which hath shewed us light: bind the sacrifice with cords,
even unto the horns of the altar" (Psalms 118:27).

jackpriests: Jack Catholic is slang for Catholic in name only; thus "jackpriests" are priests in name
only.

(Exile continued from 75)

of the sexual experiences narrated in it.

These early conflicts with "the Censor" were largely responsible for Joyce's growing sense of
persecution for his revolutionary ideas, and this became the primary motivation for his decision
to leave Ireland for Paris in 1902. Exile became a badge of honor. He did eventually return but
censorship led to a second exile, this time when he was "usurped," ejected from his residence
in the Martello tower. As he wrote to his brother Stanislaus, "I have come to accept my present
situation as a voluntary exile." In the novel *Portrait of the Artist*, Stephen Dedalus proclaims: "I will
not serve that in which I no longer believe whether it call itself my home, my fatherland or my
church: and I will try to express myself in some mode of life or art as freely as I can and as wholly
as I can, using for my defense the only arms I allow myself to use—silence, exile, and cunning."
His final exile came in 1912 when *Dubliners* was deemed "anti-Irish." Maunsel & Co finally refused
to publish it, but offered to sell Joyce the galley sheets, which were in the hands of the printer.
When Joyce went to retrieve them, the printer refused to allow such an "unpatriotic work" to be
distributed and burned them. Devastated, Joyce left Ireland that night; he would never set foot
there again.

His first two "self-exiles" had been tentative—there was always the possibility of return. In
their memoir *Our Friend James Joyce*, Mary and Padraic Colum wrote: "It is from the time of that
departure from Dublin in 1912 that the word 'exile' in the sense of 'banishment' came to be used
by Joyce as something . . . that leads to creativeness. 'I go to encounter for the millionth time the
reality of experience and to forge in the smithy of my soul the uncreated conscience of my race.'
That was not said by Stephen Hero, whose book was written in Dublin, but by Stephen Dedalus
after his final departure from Ireland."

Joyce was accustomed to having his work censored, and even banned outright, and it would be
naive to think the effect of censorship on the writing of *Ulysses* had an impact only after the fact.
His use of obscenities, blasphemies, and slurs upon the royal family were always part of his work,
as he thumbed his nose at those who attempted to keep real life out of art. As Stephen Dedalus
declared in *Portrait*: "This race and this country and this life produced me. I shall express myself
as I am." Stephen also says that the impersonality of the artist is an integral part of dramatic
art. "The artist, like the God of the creation, remains within or behind or beyond or above his
handiwork, invisible, refined out of existence, indifferent, paring his fingernails."

And at the same instant perhaps a priest round the corner is elevating it. **Dringdring**! And two streets off another locking it into a pyx. Dringadring! And in a ladychapel another taking housel all to his own cheek. Dringdring! Down, up, forward, back. **Dan Occam** thought of that, **invincible doctor. A misty English morning** the imp **hypostasis tickled his brain.** Bringing his host down and kneeling he heard twine with his second bell the first bell in the transept (he is lifting his) and, rising, heard (now I am lifting) their two bells (he is kneeling) twang in diphthong.

Cousin Stephen, you will never be a saint. Isle of saints. You were awfully holy, weren't you? You prayed to the Blessed Virgin that you might not have a red nose. You prayed to the devil in Serpentine avenue that the fubsy widow in front might lift her clothes still more from the wet street. *O si, certo!* Sell your soul for that, do, dyed rags pinned round a squaw. More tell me, more still!! On the top of *the Howth tram* alone crying to the rain: *Naked women!* naked women! What about that, eh?

What about what? What else were they invented for?

Reading two pages apiece of seven books every night, eh? I was young. You bowed to yourself in the mirror, stepping forward to applause earnestly, striking face. Hurray for the Goddamned idiot! Hray! No-one saw: tell no-one. Books you were going to write with letters for titles. Have you read his F? O yes, but I prefer Q. Yes, but W is wonderful. O yes, W.

James Joyce

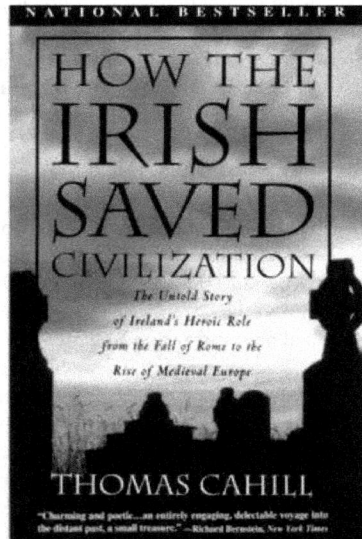

Thomas Cahill's best selling book

Fat kidneys of wheat: God's generosity to Jacob is celebrated in the Song of Moses: "And he made him to suck honey out of the rock, and oil out of the flinty rock: Butter of kine [cows], and milk of sheep, with fat of lambs, and rams of the breed of Bashan, and goats, with the fat of kidneys of wheat; and thou didst drink the pure blood of the grape" (Dueteronomy 32:13-14). [From the time Bashan was reconquered by Jehoash (2 Kings 13:25), who overcame the Syrians in three battles, according to the prophecy of Elisha Bashan almost disappears from history, although we read of the wild cattle of its rich pastures (Ezekiel 39:18; Psalms 22:12), the oaks of its forests (Isaiah 2:13; Ezekiel 27:6; Zechariah 11:2), the beauty of its extensive plains (Amos 4:1;[3] Jeremiah 50:19), and the rugged majesty of its mountains (Psalm 68:15). Soon after the conquest, the name "Gilead" was given to the whole country beyond Jordan.

Dringdring: During the celebration of the Mass a bell (the sacring bell) is rung several times, at the Sanctus, at the elevation of the host (as here), and at the Communion (when the celebrant used also to genuflect).

Dan Occam: William of Occam (1285-1389), philosopher, teologian, and Franciscan monk, originated the "law of parsimony", also called Occam's Razor, the problem-solving principle that the simplest solution tends to be the right one. He also argued that the body of Christ was not present in the host in quality or quantity, but merely in "faith," thus there is only one body of Christ no matter how many celerations of the eucharist take place simultaneously. "Hypostasis": the whole person of Christ combining human and divine natures.

invincible doctor: Occam was given the epithet *doctor singularis et invincibilis*.

A misty English morning: From the nursery rhyme: "One misty moisty morning, / When cloudy was the weather, / I chanced to meet an old man, / Clothed all in leather. / he began to compliment, / And I began to grin: / How do you do, and how do you do, / And how do you do again."

hypostasis: The whole personality of Christ as against his two natures: human and divine. As a matter of faith, the whole person of Christ is indivisibly present in the consecrated.

Cousin Stephen, you will never be a saint: After the comment on Swift by John Dryden (1631-1700): Cousin Swift, you will never be as poet."

Isle of saints: A medieval epithet for Ireland that recalls the key role played by Irish churchmen and missionaries in western European Christianity after the fall of Rome. See the book: How the Irish Saved Civilization by Thomas Cahill which covers the period from the fall of Rome to the rise of Charlemagne—the "dark ages"—during which learning, scholarship, and culture disappeared from the European continent. Cahill shows how the great heritage of western civilization—from the Greek and Roman classics to Jewish and Christian works—would have been utterly lost were it not for the holy men and women of unconquered Ireland. Far from the barbarian despoliation of the continent, monks and scribes laboriously, lovingly, even playfully preserved the west's written treasures. With the return of stability in Europe, these Irish scholars were instrumental in spreading learning. Thus the Irish not only were conservators of civilization, but became shapers of the medieval mind, putting their unique stamp on western culture.

Remember your epiphanies on green oval leaves: Stephen defines epiphany in Joyce's novel *Stephen Hero* as "a sudden spiritual manifestation" of the essence of a thing; from the Feast of the Epiphany (Jan 6), the celebration of the "showing forth" to the Magi of the body of God in the form of the infant Jesus. Joyce wrote hundreds of short epiphanies which were later incorporated into the short stories in Dubliners and his autobiographical novel Portrait of the Artist as a Young Man. His novel *Stephen Hero* was abandoned, and much of it was later incorporated into *Portrait of the Artist*.

Remember your **epiphanies** written on green oval leaves, deeply deep, copies to be sent if you died to all the great libraries of the world, including **Alexandria**? Someone was to read them there after a few thousand years, a **mahamanvantara**. **Pico della Mirandola** like. Ay, **very like a whale**. When one reads these strange pages of one long gone one feels that **one is at one with one who once** . . . .

The grainy sand had gone from under his feet. His boots trod again a damp crackling mast, razorshells, squeaking pebbles, **that on the unnumbered pebbles beats,**

Walter Pater

Pico della Mirnandola

Before having written any of his stories or poems, Joyce was already assuming these short **"ephi-phanies"** would cement his reputation and instructed his brother Stanislaus to send copies of the manuscript to "all the great libraries of the world, including **Alexandria**: the greatest and most famous library of the ancient world, which was severely damaged by fire when Julius Caesar was besieged there in 47 B.C., and finally destroyed completely by another fire during the Arab conquest of Egypt in A.D. 641.

mahamanvantara: Hindu: "great year"—a "Day of Brahma," or a thousand maha-yugas. Each maha-yuga is 4,320,000 years, so a Day of Brahma is 4,320 million years, or the time between asking someone "will you still love me tomorrow," and the time it takes them to respond by saying, "Yes, I will, yes."

[Giovanni] Pico della Mirandola (1463-94), Italian Renaissance nobleman, humanist, philosopher, and scholar who attempted to blend Christian theology with cabbalistic and pre-Christian philosophy. He had a flair for presenting and publicizing his ideas, which were often obscure and esoteric. He titled his theses on religion, philosophy, natural philosophy, and magic, *On Everything That Can Be Known*, and was described in his nephew's biography as "full of pryde and desyrous of glory and mannes prayse." Historian Charles Schmitt claims that the nephew's biography was an attempt "to destroy what his uncle had built." Pico is most famous for the events of 1486, when, at the age of 23, he went to Rome to defend his *900 Theses* against all comers, for which he wrote an accompanying book, the *Oration on the Dignity of Man*, which has been called the "Manifesto of the Renaissance" and a key text of Renaissance humanism and of what has been called the "Hermetic Reformation." He even said at the end of the book that to anyone who would like to travel to Rome to debate his *Theses*, "the disputer promises to pay the travel expenses from his own funds." Once in Rome, according to his nephew, he "converynged to make a shew of his connynge (& lytel considering how grete envye he sholde reyse agaynst hymelfe)" and was subjected to humiliation and partial defeat. Joyce is here comparing Stephen's pretensions at such an early age to Pico's. For what it's worth, Pico's *900 Theses* was the first printed book to be universally banned by the Church and nearly all copies were burned. Pico eventually became a follower of Savonarola, destroyed his own poetry, and gave away his fortune. In 1494, at the age of 31, he was poisoned under mysterious circumstances along with his friend Angelo Poliziano.

Ay, very like a whale: Polonius's ready agreement to Hamlet's "mad" demonstration ("camel" . . . weasel . . . whale") of the Protean form of a cloud (III.ii.399).

When one reads . . . one who once: Echoes the style of an essay by Walter Pater (1839-94), "Pico della Mirandola," in his famous book of essays, *The Renaissance* (1873). Pater is regarded as one of the great literary stylists. His works on Renaissance subjects were popular but controversial, reflecting his lost belief in Christianity. His much quoted maxim, "All art constantly aspires towards the condition of music," has influenced the way critical essays approach the discussion of literary works. Pater has often been depicted as the typical English aesthete, satirized as much for his prose style and critical method as for his Epicurean ideas, which often upset the more prim Victorian readers. Pater believed it was only by cultivating a passion for the arts that we could "stave off the sense of transience." What is success in life, he asked: "To burn," he answered, "always with this hard, gem-like flame, to maintain this ecstasy."

that on the unnumbered pebbles beats: in King Lear, Gloucester, blind and broken in spirit, wants to commit suicide by throwing himself from Dover Cliff. Edgar, his son but in disguise, tricks his father into believing that the level beach is indeed the top of the cliff: "The murmuring surge / That on the unnumbered pebbles chafes / Cannot be heard so high" (IV.vi.20-22).

---

wood sieved by the shipworm, **lost Armada. Unwholesome sandflats waited to suck his treading soles, breathing upward sewage breath,** a pocket of seaweed smouldered in seafire under a midden of man's ashes. He coasted them, walking warily. A porterbottle stood up, stogged to its waist, in the cakey sand dough. A sentinel: isle of dreadful thirst. Broken hoops on the shore; at the land a maze of dark cunning nets; farther away chalkscrawled backdoors and on the higher beach a dryingline with two crucified shirts. **Ringsend**: wigwams of brown steersmen and master mariners. Human shells.

He halted. I have **passed the way to aunt Sara's.** Am I not going there? Seems not. No-one about. He turned northeast and crossed the firmer sand towards the **Pigeonhouse**.

—*Qui vous a mis dans cette fichue position?*
—*C'est le pigeon, Joseph.*

St. Patrick's Church, Ringsend

View of Ringsend with South Lotts in foreground; Shelbourne Park and out to Poolbeg can be seen.

lost Armada: The Spanish Armada, after its defeat in 1588 in the English Channel, sailed north in an attempt to circle the British Isles and escape back to Spain. The fleet was scattered by storms, and many of the ships were wrecked on the coasts of Ireland and Scotland.

Unwholesome sandflats . . . breathing upward sewage breath: Much of Dublin's sewage was emptied untreated into the Liffey and its tributaries, so the streams in the metropolis were little better than open sewers, and the inshore waters of Dublin Bay, particularly just south of the mouth of the Liffey, where Stephen is walking, were notoriously polluted. Dublin had a long-delayed and controversial project for an adequate sewage system. The Main Drainage Committee's duties had been absorbed by the Improvements Committee late in 1903. The Dublin Main Drainage Works was finally inaugurated on September 24, 1906.

stogged: stalled in mire or mud.

Ringsend: (Irish: An Rinn) was originally a long narrow peninsula separated from the rest of Dublin by the then much broader estuary of the River Dodder. On early maps its name is given as "Ring's Ende" and the nearest settlements to it are given the names Merryon (Merrion) and Donny Brook. Formerly the point where ships arriving from across the Irish Sea would dock, it went into decline in the 19th and 20th centuries. The English having moved the Irish outside the city walls started referring to the area towards the Ringsend peninsula as an "Irishtown," including the building of York and Pidgeon House Roads and the Great South Wall (South Bull Wall), and development in the 16th and 17th centuries, out to the Poolbeg Lighthouse, led to an expansion of the area.

Am I not going there?: Stephen only imagined his visit to Aunt Sarah's.

Pigeonhouse: Formerly as hexagonal fort ("an apology for a battery"), now the Dublin electricity and power station, located on a breakwater that projects out into Dublin Bay as a continuation of the south bank of the Liffey. The dove, related to the pigeon, is also a traditional symbol of the Holy Ghost.

Qui vous a mis . . . le pigeon, Joseph. French: "Who has put you in this wretched condition? / It's the pigeon, Joseph." From *La Vie de Jésus* by Léo Taxil (Paris, 1884). Taxil was the pseudonym of Gabriel Jogand-Pages (1854-1907), who wrote several comically blasphemous volumes. In chapter 5, "Où Joseph, après l'avoir trouvé mauvaise, en prend son parti" (In which Joseph, having discovered evil, takes a stand), Taxil facetiously describes Joseph with his suspicions aroused: "Could he imagine, this good man of naive soul, that a pigeon had been his only rival?" Joseph then confronts Mary in response to her assertion that no man had been allowed to touch as much as her fingertips: "Ta, ta, ta, je ne prends pas des vessies pour les lanterns . . . Qui donc, se ce n'est un homme, vous a mes dans cette position?" (Tsk, tsk, tsk, I don't mistake bladers for lanterns. . . . Who in the world, if it wasn't a man, has put you in this wretched condition?); and Mary replies, "C'est le pigeon, Joseph!" Taxil cites Matthew 1 for evidence of this "incident," and suggests that it is unfortunate that the Gospel has omitted the text of these "recriminations" (Gifford and Seidman, *Ulysses Annotated*).

Patrice, home on furlough, lapped warm milk with me in the **bar MacMahon**. Son of **the wild goose, Kevin Egan** of Paris. My father's a bird, he lapped the sweet *lait chaud* with pink young tongue, plump bunny's face. Lap, *lapin*. He hopes to win in the *gros lots*. About the nature of women he read in **Michelet**. But he must send me *La Vie de Jesus* by **M. Leo Taxil**. Lent it to his friend.

—*C'est tordant*, vous savez. Moi, je suis socialiste. Je ne crois pas en l'existence de Dieu. Faut pas le dire a mon père.

—*Il croit?*

—*Mon père, oui.*

Schluss. He laps.

My Latin quarter hat. God, we simply must dress the character. I want puce gloves. You were a student, weren't you? Of what in the other devil's name? Paysayenn. P. C. N., you know: *physiques, chimiques et naturelles*. Aha. Eating your groatsworth of *mou en civet*, fleshpots of Egypt, elbowed by belching cabmen.

Jules Michelet

Van Gogh inscribed this painting Sorrow with the words **comment se fait-il qu 'il ait sur la terre une femme seule?** *("How can there be on earth a woman alone, abandoned?") from Michelet's* **La Femme.**

Patrice . . . Son of the wild goose, Kevin Eagan: "Wild geese" are Irish who, having supported the losing Stuart cause in the battle against William III of England who defeated James II at the Battle of the Boyne (1690). chose exile instead rather than live in an Ireland ruled by England. The portrait of Kevin Eagan resembles that of John Casey, Fenian imprisoned for his part in the (1867) rescue of two Fenians from a police van in Manchester; he was in Clerkenwell Prison when the Fenians made another ill-fated attempt at rescue by exploding a keg of gunpowder at the base of the prison wall, killing twelve Londoners and a police sergeant, sparking widespread public outrage.

the bar MacMahon: Named for one of the descendants of the "Wild Geese," Marie Edmé Patrice Maurice de MacMahon, duke of Magenta (1808-93), marshal of France, and second president of the Third Republic (1873-79). His military career, though, was marred by his responsibility for a series of costly defeats in the Franco-Prussian War (1870-71) that led to the French army's collapse.

lait chaud: French: "warm milk."

lapin: French: "rabbit."

the *gros lots*: French: first prize in a lottery.

Michelet: French historian Jules Michelet (1798-1874), "of the romantic school," is noted not for his objectivity but for his picturesque, impressionistic, and emotional masterpiece, *History of France* in 19 volumes, the great work of his life. Michelet was the first historian to use and define the word Renaissance. His books are considered by most modern historians "literary masterpieces, noted for their aphoristic style. There are a handful of historians whose writings fall under the category of "literary" masterpieces, including Macaulay's *History of England*, Rank's *History of the Reformation in Germany*, Burkhardt's *The Civilization of the Renaissance in Italy*, Henry Adams' *History of the United States During the Jefferson and Adams Administrations* as well as his eloquently classic *Monte-Saint-Michele and Chartres*, Momsen's *History of Rome*, Huizinga's *The Waning of the Middle Ages*, Wedgewood's *Thirty Years War*, Pirenne's *History of Belgium*, Gibbon's *Decline and Fall of the Roman Empire*, Churchill's *The Gathering Storm*, and many others deserving of mention if I had more space here. In *La Femme*—presumably the book Patrice has been reading, Michelet traces woman's growth and "education" toward her ideal and eventual role: "Woman is a religion" and her function is "to *harmonize* religion" just as "her evident vocation is love." Woman will become "superior to man" to the point where he is "strong" but she is "divine, practical, and spiritual."

La Vie de Jésus: Léo Taxil was the pseudonym of Gabriel Jogand-Pages (1854-1907), who wrote several such comically blasphemous volumes.

"Wild Geese" were Irish expatriates who chose to live in exile rather than suffer English rule.

Kevin Eagen was based on John Casey, Fenian imprisoned for his part in the rescue of two Fenians from a police van in Manchester; he was in Clerkenwell Prison when the Fenians used dynamite (killing twelve Londoners) in an attempt to destroy the wall and rescue those inside.

C'est tordant, vous savez: "It's a scream, you know. Myself, I'm a socialist. I don't believe in the existence of God. Don't tell my father" "He believes?" "My father? Yes."

Schluss: German "Enough!"

puce gloves: in Episode 1, Stephen is wearing puce gloves and green boots, an idiosyncratic costume associated with late-nineteenth century decadence and aestheticism.

mou en civet: very cheap stew.

fleshpots of Egypt: From *Exodus* 16:2-3: they wish to return to Egypt "when we sat by the flesh pots, and when we did eat bread to the full."

Just say in the most natural tone: when I was in Paris; *boul' Mich'*, I used to. Yes, used to carry punched tickets to prove an alibi if they arrested you for murder somewhere. Justice. On the night of the seventeenth of February 1904 the prisoner was seen by two witnesses. Other fellow did it: other me. Hat, tie, overcoat, nose. *Lui, c'est moi.* You seem to have enjoyed yourself.

Proudly walking. Whom were you trying to walk like? Forget: a dispossessed. With mother's money order, eight shillings, the banging door of the post office slammed in your face by the usher. Hunger toothache. *Encore deux minutes.* Look clock. Must get. *Fermé.* Hired dog! Shoot him to bloody bits with a bang shotgun, bits man spattered walls all brass buttons. Bits all khrrrrklak in place clack back. Not hurt? O, that's all right. Shake hands. See what I meant, see? O, that's all right. Shake a shake. O, that's all only all right.

You were going to do wonders, what? **Missionary to Europe after fiery Columbanus**. **Fiacre** and **Scotus** on their creepystools in heaven spilt from their pintpots, loudlatinlaughing: *Euge! Euge!* **Pretending to speak broken English** as you dragged your valise, porter threepence, across the slimy pier at Newhaven. *Comment?* Rich booty you brought back; Le Tutu, five tattered numbers of **Pantalon Blanc et Culotte Rouge**, a blue French telegram, curiosity to show:

—Mother dying come home father.

The aunt thinks you killed your mother. That's why she won't.

*Then here's a health to **Mulligan's aunt***
And I'll tell you the reason why.
She always kept things decent in
The Hannigan famileye.

His feet marched in sudden proud rhythm over the sand furrows, along by the boulders of the south wall. He stared at them proudly, piled stone mammoth skulls. Gold light on sea, on sand, on boulders. The sun is there, the slender trees, the lemon houses.

Paris rawly waking, crude sunlight on her lemon streets. Moist pith of **farls of bread**, the **froggreen wormwood**, her matin incense, court the air. **Belluomo** rises from the bed of his wife's lover's wife, the kerchiefed housewife is astir, a saucer of acetic acid in her hand. In Rodot's Yvonne and Madeleine newmake their tumbled beauties, shattering with gold teeth *chaussons* of pastry, their mouths yellowed with the *pus of flan breton*. Faces of Paris men go by, their **wellpleased pleasers**, curled **conquistadores**.

Boul' Mich': Slangy Paris contraction of Boulevard Saint-Michel, a street on the left bank of the Seine in Paris and the café center of student and bohemian life at the turn of the century. Arthur Symons (1865-1945), in "The Decadent Movement in Literature" (1893), speaks of the "noisy, brainsick young people who haunt the brasseries [beer shops] of the Boulevard Saint-Michel and exhaust their ingenuities in theorizing over the works they cannot write."

Lui, c'est moi: French: "I am he." This is a parody of Louis XIV's "L'état, c'est moi" (The State, that's me! [I am the State!]).

Encore deux minutes: French: "still two minutes left."

Fermé. French: "closed." When Joyce arrived in Paris on his first trip before his mother died, it was late and he wasn't able to convert his money into francs.

Missionary to Europe after fiery Columbanus: an Irish saint and writer whom Joyce mentions in his essay "Ireland, Island of Saints and Sages" (1907). Supposedly, in going as a missionary to Europe, Columbanus left his mother against her will. He is notable for founding a number of monasteries from around 590 in the Frankish and Lombard kingdoms, most notably Luxeuil Abbey in present-day France and Bobbio Abbey in present-day Italy. Most of what we know about Columbanus is based on his own works (as far as they have been preserved) and Jonas of Bobbio's *Vita Columbani* (Life of Columbanus), which was written between 639 and 641

St. Fiacre was a 7th-century saint, **John Duns Scotus** (1266-1308) was a Scholastic. They are generally considered to be three of the most important philosopher-theologians of the High Middle Ages (together with Thomas Aquinas and William of Ockham). The doctrines for which Scotus is best known are the "univocity of being," that existence is the most abstract concept we have, and the idea of *haecceity*, the property supposed to be in each individual thing that makes it an individual. Scotus also developed a complex argument for the existence of God, and argued for the Immaculate Conception of Mary.

Creepy stool: a 3-legged chair of repentance.

Euge! "Well done."

Newhaven: He pretended he couldn't speak the language so he could avoid tipping the porters.

Pantalon....Rouge. White Shorts and Red Pants (though *culotte rouge* is also slang for a camp follower). Joyce seems to be invoking a variant of a light Parisian magazine, *La Vie en Coulette Rouge* (Life in Red Pants, or Among the Camp Followers.

a blue French telegram: "Mother dying come home father": The telegram actually read "Nother dying," a mistake, thus a "curiosity to show."

The aunt thinks you killed your mother: In Episode 1, Buck Mulligan tells Stephen that his refusal to kneel at his mother's beside is what killed his mother. Stephen thinks: no, the cancer did.

"Matthew Hannigan's Aunt": after a song by Percy French (1854-1920). 2nd verse: "For when young lovers came / and axed her to be theirs / Mat Hannigan's aunt took each gallant, / and fired him down the stairs."

Farls: scones or small cakes.

froggreen wormwood: Absinthe.

Belluomo: handsome man, but also slang for prankster.

chaussons: puff pastry; *flan breton*: a custard tart.

Well-pleased pleasers: pleasers is a literal translation of the French word *favoris*: "sideburns. "

conquistadores: French slang for "lady-killers."

Noon slumbers. Kevin Egan rolls gunpowder cigarettes through fingers **smeared with printer's ink, sipping his green fairy as Patrice his white**. About us gobblers fork spiced beans down their gullets. *Un demi setier!* A jet of coffee steam from the burnished caldron. She serves me at his beck. *Il est irlandais. Hollandais? Non fromage. Deux irlandais, nous, Irlande, vous savez ah, oui!* She thought you wanted a cheese hollandais. Your **postprandial**, do you know that word? Postprandial. There was a fellow I knew once in Barcelona, queer fellow, used to call it his postprandial. Well: *slainte!* Around the slabbed tables the tangle of wined breaths and grumbling gorges. His breath hangs over our saucestained plates, the green fairy's fang thrusting between his lips. Of Ireland, the Dalcassians, of hopes, conspiracies, of Arthur Griffith, now, A E, pimander, good shepherd of men. To yoke me as his yokefellow, our crimes our common cause. You're your father's son. I know the voice. His fustian shirt, sanguineflowered, trembles its Spanish tassels at his secrets. **M. Drumont**, famous journalist, Drumont, know what he called queen Victoria? Old hag with the yellow teeth. *Vieille ogresse with the dents jaunes*. **Maud Gonne**, beautiful woman, *La Patrie*, **M. Millevoye**, **Felix Faure**, know how he died?

L'Absinthe by Edgar Degas

smeared with ink: Joseph Casey, the real Fenian after whom Egan was drawn, was a typesetter on the *New York Herald* of Paris.

sipping his green fairy as Patrice his white: "Green fairy's fang" is slang for absinthe, which traditionally has a natural green colour and is often referred to in historical literature as "la fée verte" (the green fairy). It is considerably more intoxicating than ordinary liquors and contains wormwood, a substance that causes deterioration of the nervous system. Absinthe originated in the canton of Neuchâtel in Switzerland in the late 18th century. It rose to great popularity as an alcoholic drink in late 19th- and early 20th-century France, particularly among Parisian artists and writers. The consumption of absinthe was opposed by social conservatives and prohibitionists, partly due to its association with bohemian culture. Absinthe drinkers included Ernest Hemingway, James Joyce, Charles Baudelaire, Paul Verlaine, Arthur Rimbaud, Henri de Toulouse-Lautrec, Amedeo Modigliani, Pablo Picasso, Vincent van Gogh, Oscar Wilde, Marcel Proust, Aleister Crowley, Erik Satie, Edgar Allan Poe, Lord Byron, and Alfred Jarry. Absinthe has often been portrayed as a dangerously addictive psychoactive drug and hallucinogen and by 1915 was banned in the United States and in much of Europe. After the banning of absinthe, Pernod Ricard was created from the Pernod Fils company, which had produced absinthe, and Pernod had a similar taste. In recent time, absinthe has not been demonstrated to be any more dangerous than ordinary spirits. Recent studies have shown that absinthe's psychoactive properties have been exaggerated, apart from that of the alcohol. A revival of absinthe began in the 1990s following the adoption of modern European Union food and beverage laws which removed long-standing barriers to its production and sale. By the early 21st century, nearly 200 brands of absinthe were being produced in a dozen countries, most notably in France, Switzerland, Australia, Spain, and the Czech Republic. You can now order both absinthe and pernod and compare the difference in taste. **White**: unlike his father, Patrice drinks milk.

Un demi setier!: A Parisian colloqualism for a *demitasse*, a small cup, but a setier is an obsolete measure for liquids, about two gallons, so asking for a small setier is like saying bring me a small gallon.

Il est Irlandais . . .: He is Irish", "Dutch?" "Not cheese. Two Irishmen, we, Ireland, you understand?" "Oh yes!"

postprandial: The term postprandial is used in many contexts. Gastronomic or social: refers to activities performed after a meal, such as drinking cocktails or smoking.

Slainte!: Gaelic: sláinte: "health."

Arthur Griffith (1872-1922), Irish nationalist, instrumental in the final achievement of Ireland's independence and founder of Sinn Féin ("To Ourselves"), the motto for various groups agitating for the revival of Irish culture and a return to Gaelic as the principal language of Ireland by disrupting the British government. With William Rooney, he founded the Celtic Literary Society and the *United Irishman*, a newspaper that crusaded for Irish independence. In 1906 he founded the newspaper *Sinn Fein*. Griffith became the first president of the newly formed Irish Free State in 1922.

M. Drummont: Edouard Adolphe (1844-1917), French journalist, editor of *La Libre Parole* (Free Speech), a virulently anti-Semitic newspaper.

Vieille ogresse . . . dents jaunes: French: "Old ogress with yellow teeth." In folklore, cannibalism turned teeth yellow.

Maude Gonne: (1866-1953) Irish nationalist, famed beauty, beloved of Yeats, refugee to Paris.

La Patrie, **M Millovoye**: French newspaper edited by Lucien Millevoye (1850-1918), lover of Maude Gonne and father of her daughter, Iseult.

Felix Faure: (1841-99) President of the French Republic (1895-99), died suddenly of a cerebral hemorrhage. Rumor current in Paris was that it was the result of "sexual excess."

Licentious men. The **froeken, *bonne à tout faire*,** who rubs male nakedness in the bath at Upsala. *Moi faire, she said, Tous les messieurs.* Not this *Monsieur*, I said. Most licentious custom. Bath a most private thing. I wouldn't let my brother, not even my own brother, most lascivious thing. **Green eyes, I see you. Fang,** I feel. Lascivious people.

The blue fuse burns deadly between hands and burns clear. Loose tobaccoshreds catch fire: a flame and acrid smoke light our corner. Raw facebones under his **peep of day boy's** hat. How **the head centre got away**, authentic version. Got up as a young bride, man, veil, orangeblossoms, drove out the road to **Malahide**. Did, faith. **Of lost leaders**, the betrayed, wild escapes. Disguises, clutched at, gone, not here.

William III ("William of Orange")
King of England, Scotland, and
Ireland

The Orange order flag incorporates
the color orange, the purple star of the
Williamites, and the St. George's Cross

The Orange Order logo

froeken: *fröken*, Swedish: "an unmarried woman." **bonne à tout faire**: French: "maid of all work." *Moi faire . . . tous les messieurs*: "I do all the gentlemen. **Green eyes, I see you: Iago to Othello**: "Oh, beware, my lord, of jealousy. / It is the green-eyed monster which doth mock / The meat it feeds on" (III.iii.165-167). **Fang**: remember? "Green fairy's fang" as slang for absinthe.

The blue fuse: The cigarettes Kevin Egan rolls remind Stephen of the fuses Egan once made for their explosives.

peep of the day boy's: Precursors of the Orangemen, late 18th-century Ulster Protestants named for their early morning raids on the cottages of Catholic peasants, whom they sought to displace from Ulster. The Orangemen regarded themselves as "an organization for the maintenance of Britih authority in Ireland." When the English Parliament came close to granting Home Rule for Ireland in 1886, it was to the tune of anti-Home Rule riots in the Orangemen's stronghold of Belfast. They trace their name to the Battle of the Boyne, held on July 1, 1690 on the banks of the Boyne River on the East coast of Ireland. It was a battle between King James VII of Scotland (seen as representing the Catholics) and James II of England and Ireland and his supporters on one side and Dutch Prince William of Orange (seen as representing the Protestants) and his followers on the other side. Prince William of Orange won the battle and became King William III. The symbolic importance of this battle has made it one of the best-known battles in the history of the British Isles and a key part of the folklore of the Orange Order. However, modern analysis of documents from the time suggests that Catholics and Protestants fought on both sides. Its commemoration today is principally by the Orange Order, which records the first commemorative parades as having been held in 1791. In recent decades, "The Twelfth" has often been marked by confrontations, as members of the Orange Order attempt to celebrate the date by marching past or through what they see as their traditional route. Some of these areas, however, now have a nationalist majority who object to marches passing through what they see as their areas. Each side thus dresses up the disputes in terms of the other's alleged attempts to repress them; Nationalists still see Orange Order marches as provocative attempts to "show who is boss," while Unionists insist that they have a right to "walk the Queen's highway." Since the start of The Troubles, the celebrations of the battle have been seen as playing a critical role in the awareness of those involved in the unionist/ nationalist tensions in Northern Ireland (v2.travelark.org).

How the head centre got away: James Stephens (1824-1901), an Irish agitator, was Chief Organizer and subsequently Head Centre of the Fenian Society (Irish Republican Brotherhood), which he created in 1858. The Fenians (nicknamed the "hillside men") took their name from the Fianna of Irish legend, a standing force of warriors under Finn MacCool in the third century. They were committed to the achievement of Irish independence through terrorist tactics and violent revolution. In November 1866 Stephens was betrayed by a spy planted in his Dublin office. He was arrested, tried, and sentenced, but a few days later he was "rescued" from Dublin's Richmond Gaol by a group of Fennians. He was smuggled out of the country and made his way to America, where he was elected Head Centre of the American branch of the Fenians. Stephens resisted pressure by many to call for immediate insurrection, and was thus denigrated by those who opposed him by spreading the apocryphal story that he assumed the disguise of a woman to effect his escape, "betraying and abandoning" his lieutenants in Ireland in the process.

Malahide: a village and seaside resort nine miles north of Dublin on the coast of the Irish sea. Stephens made his escape to sea by this route.

Of lost leaders . . . Robert Browning: (1812-1889), "The Lost Leader" (1845) in which he laments the once-radical Wordsworth's increasing conservatism on being given a government pension in 1842 and made Poet Laureate in 1843. "Just for a handful of silver he left us, / Just for a riband to stick in his coat."

Spurned lover. I was a strapping young **gossoon** at that time, I tell you. I'll show you my likeness one day. I was, faith. Lover, for her love he prowled with colonel **Richard Burke, tanist of his sept, under the walls of Clerkenwell** and, crouching, saw a flame of vengeance hurl them upward in the fog. Shattered glass and toppling masonry. In gay Paree he hides, Egan of Paris, unsought by any save by me. Making his day's stations, the dingy printingcase, his three taverns, the **Montmartre** lair he sleeps short night in, **rue de la Goutte d'Or, damascened with flyblown faces of the gone.** Loveless, landless, wifeless. She is quite nicey comfy without her outcast man, madame in **rue Git-le-Coeur,** canary and two buck lodgers. Peachy cheeks, a zebra skirt, frisky as a young thing's. Spurned and undespairing. Tell Pat you saw me, won't you? . . .

La rue de la Charbonnière and la rue de la Goutte d'Or

The Goutte d'Or and the Damascended Faces of the Gone
The Golden Drop—from Emile Zola's gone faces layering one into another, to the taverns of Montmarte that Joyce frequented, to the expats of the '50s and '60s, to the African immigrants of the 2000s, this enclave at the bottom of the hill has served writers and artists for centuries. James Baldwin sipped coffee and smoked cigarettes in the little shops in the Goutte d'Or, a community in Montmarte also known as Little Africa. Langston Hughes frequented the jazz joints and smoky cafes as a young poet. From one of the alleyways, you might still catch a long-ago echo of Josephine Baker doing her banana dance, as she became the toast of the City of Light. This hilly, crowded community in Paris's 18th arrondissement (or district) is called Goutte d'Or, or the Shower of Gold, or The Golden Drop, or the Golden Liquor. Today, it's more often referred to as Little Africa. When I was last in Paris, I checked it out one hot afternoon, hoping some of the history would rub off on me. Down one alley, I came upon Marche Dejean, a sumptuous, exotic open-air market that strikes you with its colors and sounds. Many of the women carried their babies in sacks tied around their backs. You could smell the gumbo, the dried fish, the plaintains, the peppers, the pineapples, the mangoes—all those spices of African life. There was a Haitian market where I got a lift from

(Goutte d'Or continued on 94)

gossoon: a boy, a servant boy, a lackey; rustic, inexperienced.

Richard Burke: a colonel in the American Civil War and an Irish American member of the Irish Republican Brotherhood, nicknamed the "Fenians." Burke led a Fenian group in the rescue of two Fenian leaders in Manchester in September 1867, was arrested for other Fenian activities, and was among other Fenian leaders who were supposed to have been freed by the abortive gunpowder plot against Clerkenwell Prison. The explosion killed 12 people and 120 were injured, but none of the prisoners escaped.

tanist of his sept: A *sept* was a medieval Irish tribal division. Among the ancient Irish, a tanist was the heir apparent to the tribal chief, elected during the chief's lifetime. The implication here is that Bruke was to be James Stephens's successor as Head Centre.

under the walls of Clerkenwell: The plot to blast the wall of the prison yard and rescue Burke and Casey hinged on their scheduled exercise time—they were supposed to crouch down against the yard's outer wall to avoid injury. But informers tipped off the warden, who changed their exercise time and foiled the plot.

Montmarte: a poor, rundown section of Paris, a favorite haunt of avant-garde artists, bohemians, and students, now the site of the beautiful Sacre Coeur Cathedral and a fashionable tourist spot. The iconic windmill marks the Moulin Rouge club famous for its can-can dancers.

rue de la Goutte d'Or, damascended with flyblown faces of the gone: This street of "the Golden Drop" or the "Golden Liquor" in Montmarte was named for the golden wine from long-since displaced vineyards. The "gone" whose faces "damascene" (the art of layering different metals one into another) the street are several of Emile Zola's (1840-1902) characters: Gervaise Macquet, the protagonist of *L'Assommoir* (1877), lives in the Goute d'Or quarter of Paris and, with her husband, declines into dereliction, filth, ananition, and finally death as a result of alcoholism. Her daughter Nana (*Nana*, 1880), en route to supreme success as a grand *cocotte* (prostitute), dies from smallpox. The second to last paragraph of *Nana* is a particularly gruesome description of her corpse, as if the "virus," with which she had "poisoned a people had crawled into her face and rotted it away." Stephen's adjective "flyblown" is mild in comparison with Zola's prose.

rue Git-le-Coeur: (Street Sacred to the Memory of the Heart) runs parallel to the Boulevard Saint-Michel, near the Seine on the Left Bank. When I first went to Paris in 1962, I was told to go there to see all the beatnik poets sitting there shooting up heroin. *(See detailed note on facing page.)*

*"The Fenian Guy Fawkes" by John Tenniel, published in **Punch** magazine, on December 28, 1867*

... I wanted to get poor Pat a job one time. *Mon fils*, soldier of France. I taught him to sing *The boys of Kilkenny are stout roaring blades*. Know that old lay? I taught Patrice that. **Old Kilkenny: saint Canice, Strongbow's castle on the Nore**. Goes like this. O, O. He takes me, **Napper Tandy**, by the hand.

O, O The boys of
Kilkenny . . .

Weak wasting hand on mine. They have forgotten Kevin Egan, not he them. **Remembering thee, O Sion**.

La bibliothèque de la Goutte d'Or and le centre
Fleury-Barbara

(Goutte d'Or continued from 92)

a ginger soda. A man was selling goods from the sidewalk, another from his car. I couldn't resist buying some books out of a small African bookshop. Art shops everywhere. Ghanaian perfume stores, Muslim butchers, Arab bakers and dozens of shops hawking artificial hair and other products. Turning down one alley, I came upon a police van parked near a Mosque that was just ending its afternoon worship. The van was a mobile station that rounds up *les sans papiers*, or people without papers, illegal immigrants. Africans are often stopped and questioned. For a moment, I thought I was in Casablanca, or at least the movie, when the police were looking for the letters of transit that had been given to Humphrey Bogart who had hidden them in the piano played by Dooley Wilson. Many of the immigrants without proper credentials were often jailed and sent home. Africans first came to France as explorers, then as *griots*—oral historians, also trained to excel as orators, storytellers, lyricists and musicians. The *griot* kept records of all the births, deaths, and marriages through the generations of the village or family. They were astrologers and entertainers establishing a long history of French and African connections. Paris didn't cease to exist once Hemingway was done with it. After World War I, legions of black expatriates flowed into Paris hoping to escape American segregation and find artistic liberty—Paul Robeson, James Baldwin, James Weldon Johnson, Chester Himes, Richard Wright, Claude McKay. If you visit "The Marble Palace," the building that housed the apartment of Josephine Baker, you can cross the street and check out the former embassy where Thomas Jefferson lived with his black girlfriend Sally Hemings. Around the corner there's the Milliardaire Cabaret, a 1920s hangout for black American musicians and entertainers after World War II. One street over, you can walk the block where jazz great Sidney Bechet opened his nightclub Chez Sidney in 1951. Take the tram to the top of Montmartre—the highest point in Paris—for that stunning view of the city. Once known as the Harlem of Paris, this area swelled with black culture before the 1950s, when blacks began to shift to the Left Bank. A large part of the mystique that Paris holds for African Americans stems from the rich literary culture that is part of their 20th-century heritage in the city where they were deeply and irrevocably influenced by the time that they spent in Paris.

Mon fils: French, "my son."

The boys of Kilkenny: Anonymous Irish song praising Kilkenny for its scenery, young men, and particularly its young women: "Oh! The boys of Kilkenny are neat roving blades, / And when ever they meet with dear little maids, / They kiss them, and coax them, and spend their money free. / Oh! Of all towns in Ireland, Kilkenny for me. / Oh! Of all towns in Ireland, Kilkenny for me."

Old Kilkenny: A county and a town on the River Nore in southeastern Ireland named after St. Canice (St. Kenny); **kil**: "church or cell."

saint Canice: (died about 599), he accompanied St. Columcille (521-97; also called St. Columba) on a mission to convert Brude, king of the Picts. Columcille, along with St. Bridgid and St. Patrick, is one of the three patron saints of Ireland. St. Canice's Cathedral (now Protestant) from the 13th century and a round tower mark the site of the 6th century monastery that gave Kilkenny its name.

Strongbow's castle on the Nore: Richard FitzGilbert, earl of Pembroke, called "Strongbow" (died 1176), was a Norman adventurer and one of the key leaders of the Anglo-Norman invasion of Ireland in 1169. His castle on the Nore was built in 1172 near the site of St. Canice's monastery to command the strategic river crossing. The nickname was given to him in the 14th Century, probably a mistranslation of the Latin word for "Strangehose," referring to the foreign leggings in war.

Napper Tandy: from "The Wearing of the Green," anonymous Irish ballad from the late 18th C., which laments Ireland "is the most distressing country that ever yet was seen, / They're hanging men and woman there for wearin' of the green." James Napper Tandy (1740-1803), revolutionary, founder of United Irishmen, supporter of the French Revolution.

Remembering thee, O Sion: A phrase of mourning, as in Psalm 137:1-2: By the rivers of Babylon, there we sat down, yea, we wept, when we remembered Zion."

If claiming that **James Napper Tandy** was a revolutionary, one must add that he was an ineffectual revolutionary. In 1793, he was forced into exile and made his way to Philadelphia and then to Paris when the French government made him a general and sent him back to Ireland to raise an army against the British. In 1798, he landed at Rutland Island, off the coast of Donega, but abandoned the venture the same day. While returning circuitously to France, he was captured in Hamburg, turned over to the British, and, at a trial in Ireland, was sentenced to death. He was released unconditionally, however, at the demand of Napoleon Bonaparte, and went to Bordeaux to live, where he died the following year (Encyclopedia Britannica).

Richard Fitzgilbert de Clare ("Strongbow")

The new air greeted him, harping in wild nerves, **wind of wild air of seeds of brightness**. Here, I am not walking out to the **Kish lightship**, am I? He stood suddenly, his feet beginning to sink slowly in the quaking soil. Turn back.

Turning, he scanned the shore south, his feet sinking again slowly in new sockets. **The cold domed room of the tower waits**. Through the barbacans the shafts of light are moving ever, slowly ever as my feet are sinking, creeping duskward over the dial floor. Blue dusk, nightfall, deep blue night. In the darkness of the dome they wait, their pushedback chairs, my obelisk valise, around a board of abandoned platters. Who to clear it? **He has the key. I will not sleep there when this night comes**. A shut door of a silent tower, entombing their— blind bodies, the panthersahib and his pointer. Call: no answer. He lifted his feet up from the suck and turned back by **the mole of boulders**. Take all, keep all. My soul walks with me, **form of forms**. So in the moon's midwatches I pace the path above the rocks, in **sable silvered, hearing Elsinore's tempting flood**.

The flood is following me. I can watch it flow past from here. Get back then by the **Poolbeg road** to the strand there. He climbed over the sedge and eely oarweeds and sat on a stool of rock, resting his ashplant in a **grike**.

A bloated carcass of a dog lay lolled on **bladderwrack**. Before him the gunwale of a boat, sunk in sand. *Un coche ensablé* **Louis Veuillot** called Gautier's prose. These heavy sands are language tide and wind have silted here. And these, the stoneheaps of dead builders, a warren of weasel rats. Hide gold there. Try it. You have some. Sands and stones. Heavy of the past. **Sir Lout's toys**. Mind you don't get one bang on the ear. I'm the bloody well gigant rolls all them bloody well boulders, bones for my **steppingstones. Feefawfum. I zmellz de bloodz odz an Iridzman**.

The tower was leased from the British War Office by Joyce's university friend Oliver St. John Gogarty (upon whom Buck Mulligan was modeled), with the purpose of "Hellenising" Ireland. Joyce stayed there for six days, from September 9th to the 14th in 1904. Gogarty later attributed Joyce's abrupt departure to a midnight incident in which Haines fired a revolver while in the throes of a nightmare in which he was being attacked by a panther. The bullets hit several pots and pans hanging on the wall above Joyce's bed. Joyce woke to the sound of gunfire and the pans crashing down upon his head.

wind of wild air of seeds of brightness: Bloom, Stephen, Buck Mulligan and several other medical students are featured In Episode 14, "Oxen of the Sun," which takes place at the Maternity Hospital in Holles Street where Mrs. Purefoy lies in labor. Stephen cites fabulous accounts of impregnation by wind as in Virgil and as in the legend of Zephryus, the west wind ("O west wind when wilt thou blow the rain can down come rain, I wish I was with my love and in my bed again"), who fathered Achilles' horses. Other myths of impregnation involve a shower of seeds from the sun or the stars or the bright sky; as Zeus in the form of a shower of gold impregnated Danaë. **The Kish lightship**: a lightship moored at the northern end of Kish Bank, two miles east of Kingstown (now Dun Laoghaire). The bank forms a dangerous obstacle at the southern entrance to Dublin Bay.

The cold domed room of the Tower waits: Stephen has been staying with Buck Mulligan and Hains at the Martello Tower, one of many small defensive forts that were built during the 19th century. Stephen is loathe to return because he fears Haines' violent nightmares. As he says at the end of the opening episode, feels he's been "usurped." **He has the key**: Stephan has given the one key to Buck Mulligan. **the mole of boulders**: The seawall topped by Poolberg Road, that extends the south bank of the Liffey east into Dublin Bay for more than two miles. The Pigeon House sits astride the wall a mile and a half in from Poolberg Light at the wall's end. **form of forms**: We're back to good ol' Aristotle. Stephen had said in the opening sentence of this episode, "thought through my eyes," but here he refers to Aristotle's *On the Soul*: "As the hand is the instrument of instruments, so the mind [*nous*, soul] is the form of forms and sensation the form of sensibles." In his *Metaphysics*, Aristotle argues that the prime mover is thought thinking on itself.

in sable silvered . . . tempting flood: Horatio reports to Hamlet about his midnight encounter with the Ghost (I.ii), and in response to one of Hamlet's questions he describes the Ghost's beard as "a sable silvered." Horatio attempts to keep Hamlet from following the Ghost, lest it be an evil spirit and tempt or deceive Hamlet into throwing himself into the sea. "What if it tempt you toward the flood, my lord, / Or to the dreadful summit of the cliff?" (I.iv.69-70).

Poolberg road: see above note on mole of boulders. **grike**: a crevice, chink, crack.

bladderwrack: a species of seaweed with air bladders in its fronds. *Un coche ensablé . . .* **prose**: French: A coach stuck in the sand." French journalist Louis Veuillot's (1813-83) description of Théophile Gautier's (1811-72) prose style. Veuillot was an ardent supporter of the Church; Gautier a romantic poet, literary critic, dramatist, and novelist. While an ardent defender of Romanticism, Gautier's work is difficult to classify and remains a point of reference for many subsequent literary traditions such as Parnassianism, Symbolism, Decadence and Modernism. He was widely esteemed by writers as disparate as Balzac, Baudelaire, Flaubert, Pound, Eliot, James, Proust and Wilde. **Louis Veuillot**: a leader of the Iltramontane party, which opposed 19th century political efforts to curtail the secular powers of the Church of Rome in France. Veuillot was a notoriously uncompromising anti-romantic (because the French romantics were traditionally anti-church). **Gautier's**: Théophile Gautier was famous for a "flamboyant" romanticism with overtones of frank hedonism and a "pagan" contempt for traditional morality. **Sir Lout's toys . . . oldz an Iridzman**: a scrambled free association that includes the nursery rhyme "Fee, fi, fo, fum, I smell the blood of an Englishman."

Steppingstones: the jumble of boulders on the beach recalls the Giant's Causeway, a great pile of basaltic pillars on the northeastern coast of Ireland. One legend accounts for the causeway by crediting it to the giant Finn McCool, who, irritated by a braggert Scottish giant, pitched the rocks into the sea so that he could cross and humiliate the Scott. Sir Lout is perhaps Joyce's creation, a prehistoric giant, sexually weak according to Joyce, who had rocks in his mouth instead of teeth.

A point, live dog, grew into sight running across the sweep of sand. Lord, is he going to attack me? Respect his liberty. You will not be master of others or their slave. I have my stick. Sit tight. From farther away, walking shoreward across from the crested tide, figures, two. **The two maries**. They have tucked it safe mong the bulrushes. Peekaboo. I see you. No, the dog. He is running back to them. Who?

Galleys of the **Lochlanns** ran here to beach, in quest of prey, their bloodbeaked prows riding low on a molten pewter surf. **Dane vikings**, torcs of tomahawks aglitter on their breasts when **Malachi wore the collar of gold**. A **school of turlehide whales** stranded in hot noon, spouting, hobbling in the shallows. Then from the starving cagework city a horde of jerkined dwarfs, my people, with flayers' knives, running, scaling, hacking in green blubbery whalemeat. **Famine, plague and slaughters**. Their blood is in me, their lusts my waves. I moved among them on **the frozen Liffey**, that I, a changeling, among the spluttering resin fires. **I spoke to no-one: none to me**.

The River Liffey was previously named An Ruirthech, meaning "fast (or strong) runner." The word Liphe (or Life) referred originally to the name of the plain through which the river ran, but eventually came to refer to the river itself. It was also known as the Anna Liffey, possibly from an anglicisation of *Abhainn na Life*, the Irish phrase that translates into English as "River Liffey" (see photo at bottom of 3). From Joyce to Radiohead, the Liffey is often referenced in literature and song: Insofar as *Finnegans Wake* has characters, the female protagonist of the novel, Anna Livia Plurabelle, is herself an allegory of the river, its first sentence being: "riverrun, past Eve and Adam's, from swerve of shore to bend of bay, brings us by a commodius vicus of recirculation back to Howth Castle and Environs." A few of the other references are:

"She asked that it be named for her. —The river took its name from the land. —the land took its name from the woman."
—Eavan Boland, *Anna Liffey*

"That there, that's not me—I go where I please—I walk through walls, I float down the Liffey—I'm not here, this isn't happening."
—Radiohead, "How to Disappear Completely"

"Somebody once said that 'Joyce has made of this river the Ganges of the literary world,' but sometimes the smell of the Ganges of the literary world is not all that literary."
—Brendan Behan, *Confessions of an Irish Rebel*

"No man who has faced the Liffey can be appalled by the dirt of another river."
—Iris Murdoch, *Under the Net*

In July 2011, a long-term homeless man rescued his pet rabbit after it had been thrown into the river, diving off O'Connell Bridge in front of hundreds of people. Videos of the rescue circulated on the internet, and the man received an honor (and job offer at an animal shelter) for his actions. The man who threw the rabbit into the river was arrested.

The two maries: Mary Magdalene and Mary the Mother of James and Joses," followers of Jesus, who in Matthew and in Mark watch at the Crucifixion, "ministering unto him" and who also watch at the sepulcher after the entombment and are then the first to receive the news, "He is not here: for he is risen" (Matthew 27-28; Mark 15-16).

Lochlanns: Gaelic: "Lake Place" or "Lake Dwellers," Irish name for the Norwegians, who constituted the first waves of the Scandinavian invasions around 787. Dane Vikings were involved in subsequent invasions. Scandinavian power was not broken until the early eleventh century.

when Malachai wore the collar of gold: from Thomas More's (1779-1852) "Let Erin Remember the Days of Old". Malachi II (948-1022), High King of Ireland, helped to free Ireland from the Norse invaders with Brian Boroimhe ("Boru", 926-1014) best known for his defeat of the Danes on Good Friday 1014, after which he was slain in his tent. Malachi took the "collar of Tomar" from the neck of a Danish chieftain whom he had defeated.

school of turlehide whales: in 1331, during a famine, a school of whales beached themselves on the shores of Dublin Bay; the Dubliners killed and ate them. The whales were from 30 to 40 feet long, so thick that men standing on each side of one of them could not see those on the other side. Upwards of 200 of them were killed.

Famine, plague and slaughters: 14th century Dublin saw all three, including the Black Plague in 1348 and the slaughters of the Bruce invasion in 1314-18 (see note below on Bruce's brother).

the frozen Liffey: in the winter of 1338-9, the Liffey froze so solidly that people played football and lit fires on it. The Liffey froze again in 1739, but Joyce is referring here to earlier event (see note in left column).

I spoke to no-one: none to me: After the English folk song: "There was a Jolly Miller / Once lived on the River Dee . . . I care for nobody; no not I / And nobody cares for me."

Sarah's Bridge on the River Liffey (1831)

*The Liffey today is spanned by numerous bridges, including the O'Connell Bridge, the Ha'Penny Bridge, the James Joyce Bridge (2003), and the Samuel Beckett Bridge (2009), the last two built by Santiago Calatrava. Art works along the river and its quays include the Famine Memorial Statues and the World Hunger Stone. The River Liffey has been used for centuries since the time of the Vikings. In the **Annals of Inisfallen** for the year 808, an entry reads "A defeat by the Laigin on Áed, son of Niall, at the river Liphé." The first bridge was built in 1014, named the Father Matthew Bridge. Prior to that, people just waded through the shallow water from one bank to the other. The most famous bridge (used only for foot traffic) is the Ha'Penny Bridge (pronounced Hap-Nee), built in 1816 out of cast-iron, so named because the price of the original toll to cross matched the fee charged by the ferry boats that the bridge replaced. (See photo at bottom of 3.)*

The dog's bark ran towards him, stopped, ran back. Dog of my enemy. I just simply **stood pale, silent, bayed about**. *Terribilia meditans*. A primrose doublet, **fortune's knave**, smiled on my fear. For that are you pining, the bark of their applause? Pretenders: live their lives. **The Bruce's brother, Thomas Fitzgerald**, silken knight, **Perkin Warbeck**, York's false scion, in breeches of silk of whiterose ivory, wonder of a day, and **Lambert Simnel**, with a tail of nans and sutlers, a scullion crowned. All kings' sons. **Paradise of pretenders** then and now.

Perkin Warbeck and Lambert Simnel: Pretenders to the Crown

In 1485 Richard III, the last Plantagenet king of England, was defeated and killed at the Battle of Bosworth ("A horse, a horse, my kingdom for a horse!"). He was the last English king to die in battle, his corpse taken to the nearby town of Leicester and buried without ceremony. Henry Tudor then ascended the throne as Henry VII. Although this was the final, decisive victory in the famous Wars of the Roses, Henry faced many challenges from powerful nobles and feudal lords who looked to influence the throne wherever possible. Should the young King prove intractable, there were always more pliant contenders to be found since his own questionable legitimacy to the throne encouraged dissent and rebellion.

Two alternative claimants appeared to the throne: Perkin Warbeck and Lambert Simnel, though it was uncertain who had the better claim. Despite Richard's death, his faction, the Yorkists, remained undefeated in spirit and were plotting Henry's overthrow. And then a convenient figurehead appeared. Lambert Simnel was presented as Richard III's nephew, the Earl of Warwick. The real Earl was a similar age to the young boy and had been imprisoned in the Tower of London. The Yorkists presented Lambert Simnel as this legitimate claimant. Lambert Simnel had a humble origin, born around 1477, making him around 10 years old at the time of the rebellion. He was trained in courtly manners and etiquette to make his disguise more convincing. A rumor was then spread that the "Earl" had escaped from prison. On May 24, Simnel was crowned King Edward VI at Christ Church Cathedral in Dublin.

An army of Irish troops and 2,000 Flemish mercenaries were defeated by Henry's troops. Henry had an unexpected trump card in his hand with which to defeat Simnel. The real Earl of Warwick, long imprisoned in the Tower, was in fact still alive. Henry was able to unmask the pretender as an imposter, and the rebellion foundered.

While this first pretender was easily suppressed, the next proved to be a serious thorn in Henry's side for much of the next decade. Perkin Warbeck claimed he was one of Edward's two sons who had been imprisoned by Richard III in the Tower. Even today it is not certain what happened to the two princes, since no bodies were ever found, but Warbeck claimed to have escaped. In 1490, Warbeck appeared at the court of Burgundy on the continent, claiming to be Richard, the younger of the two princes. Warbeck explained that Edward V, his older brother, had indeed been killed, but that he was spared due to his young age. Warbeck also claimed he had been forced to take an oath not to reveal his identity for some years, in return for being spared. He had stayed in Europe under the protection of Yorkist loyalists from 1483 to 1490 but now intended to return to England, having received support from the French king and the sister of Edward IV, his supposed aunt, who probably knew he was an imposter but stood to benefit if he gained the throne. Even several members of the English nobility threw their lot in with Warbeck. But the plan failed. The nobles were executed and Henry crushed the invading

(Pretenders continued on facing page)

stood pale, silent, bayed about: Stephen as Actaeon who, having spied on Diana bathing, was turned into a stag hunted by his own dogs. The deer is also a traditional symbol of the hidden secret of the self. Joyce uses the image of the disdainful stag flashing his antlers at the rabble in his poem "The Holy Office" (1904), a scabrous piece in 100 lines blasting the self-satisfaction of the literary nationalists, his first angry response to the efforts of his contemporaries—which he was unable to publish, so he published it himself as a broadside:

> Where they have crouched
> and crawled and prayed
> I stand, the self-doomed, unafraid,
> Unfellowed, friendless and alone,
> Indifferent as the herring-bone,
> Firm as the mountain-ridges where
> I flash my antlers on the air.

Terribilia meditans. Latin: meditating on terrible things.

fortune's knave: Rosencrantz and Guildenstern describe themselves to Hamlet as fortune's "privates" (II.ii.238), and they are, of course, at least dupes if not knaves. Cleopatra also invokes the meaninglessness of high rank after Antony's death: "'Tis paltry to be Caesar. / Not being Fortune, he's but Fortune's knave, / A minister of her will" (V.ii.2-4).

The Bruce's brother . . . Paradise of pretenders: references to those who made attempts to claim either the Irish or the English throne. Joyce, calling Ireland a "paradise of pretenders" because it was all too ready to entertain the ambitions of those who would challenge English monarchy: Robert "the Outlaw King" Bruce was King of the Scots from 1306 to his death in 1329. One of the most renowned warriors of his generation, he eventually led Scotland during the First War of Scottish independence against English rule, winning the decisive Battle of Bannockburn (1314) and ultimately confirming Scottish independence in the Treaty of Northampton (1328). In the film *Braveheart*, he is portrayed as having betrayed William Wallace (played by Mel Gibson), but there's no historical evidence Bruce was at Falkirk, although he did switch sides several times in these early years.

Edward Bruce (d. 1318), Robert freed Scotland from the English at Bannockburn in 1314 after which Edward invaded Ireland and attempted to establish himself king—only to be slain by the Irish.

Thomas Fitzgerald (1513-37), tenth earl of Kildare, also known as "Silkin Thomas," raised a rebellion against Henry VIII, defeated and executed on Tyburn.

Perkin Warbeck (1474-99), a commoner and Yorkist pretender to the throne by claiming to be Richard, Duke of York, son of Edward IV (and one of the two young princes supposedly murdered by Richard III), supported by the Anglo-Irish lords of Ireland—eventually executed at Tyburn.

Lambert Simnel (1475-1525), son of an Irish baker, trained by Yorkists to impersonate the Earl of Warwick in attempt to overthrow Henry VII, crowned in Dublin (1487) as Edward VI, invaded England, was captured and used by Henry as scullion in his kitchens.

(Pretenders continued from facing page)

army before Warbeck even got off his ship. Forced to flee, Warbeck was welcomed by James IV of Scotland. He married Lady Catherine Gordon, daughter of George Gordon, and with this alliance came strong Scottish support. In 1496 Warbeck and James IV crossed into England. The invasion was disastrous as Warbeck failed to find the hoped-for public support in England. And

(Pretenders continued on 102)

He saved men from drowning **and you shake at a cur's yelping. But the courtiers who mocked Guido** in Or san Michele were in their own house. House of . . . We don't want any of your medieval abstrusiosities. Would you do what he did? A boat would be near, a lifebuoy. Natürlich, put there for you. Would you or would you not? The man that was drowned nine days ago off **Maiden's rock**. They are waiting for him now. The truth, spit it out. I would want to. I would try. I am not a strong swimmer. Water cold soft. When I put my face into it in **the basin at Clongowes. Can't see! Who's behind me?** Out quickly, quickly! Do you see the tide flowing quickly in on all sides, sheeting the lows of sand quickly, shellcocoacoloured? If I had land under my feet. I want his life still to be his, mine to be mine. A drowning man. His human eyes scream to me out of horror of his death. I... With him together down... I could not save her. Waters: bitter death: lost.

A woman and a man. I see her skirties. Pinned up, I bet.

(Pretenders continued from 101)

when Henry offered James his daughter in marriage, the offer was accepted and Scottish support for the pretender melted away. James sent Warbeck back to Ireland in a ship called the *Cuckoo*, a signal perhaps that Warbeck's fraud was revealed.

Warbeck made two more attempts to invade England and defeat Henry. Both attempts ended in failure, with a panic-stricken Warbeck's surrender and capture. His confession is an adventure novel in itself. He was born in 1474 to John Osbeck, the comptroller of the city of Tournai in Belgium, and Katherine de Faro. At the age of 10, Perkin was learning Dutch, and then he learned from various masters before finding employment with John Strewe, an English merchant. Then he traveled several countries, before a Breton merchant hired him and brought him to Cork, Ireland, in 1491, where he learned to speak English. After he was seen wearing silk clothes, some Cork citizens honored him as a member of the Royal House of York. This led to the decision to claim that he was the younger son of King Edward IV. After the confession, Henry provided Warbeck accommodation at the court, his wife becoming handmaid to Henry's queen. Eight months later, Warbeck tried to escape and was soon recaptured. Imprisoned in the Tower, he was hanged as a commoner in 1499.

Lambert Simnel fared much better. Since he was only a child when the rebellion occurred, he was given a job in King Henry's kitchen. Later he became a falconer for the king, and never showed the slightest inclination to rebel again.

Mary Shelley (author of *Frankenstein*) wrote a historical novel, *The Fortunes of Perkin Warbeck: A Romance,* which takes the Yorkist point of view. Shelley proceeds from the conceit that Perkin Warbeck died in childhood and the supposed impostor was indeed Richard of Shrewsbury. Henry VII of England is repeatedly described as a "fiend" who hates Elizabeth of York, his wife and Richard's sister, and the future Henry VIII, mentioned only twice in the novel, is a vile youth who abuses dogs. Her preface establishes that records of the Tower of London, as well as the histories of Edward Hall, Raphael Holinshed (upon whose "Chronicles" Shakespeare based many of his history plays), Francis Bacon, and the letters of Sir John Ramsay to Henry VII that are printed in the Appendix to John Pinkerton's *History of Scotland* established this as fact. Influenced by the novels of Sir Walter Scott, Shelley believed that Warbeck really was Richard and had escaped from the Tower of London. She endows his character with elements of Percy Shelley, her husband, the great poet, portraying Warbeck sympathetically as "an angelic essence, incapable of wound," who is led by his sensibility onto the political stage (historicmysteries.com).

He saved men from drowning: Stephen is thinking of Buck Mulligan here, who saved a man from drowning.

But the courtiers ... House of Guido: Guido Cavalcanti (1250-1300), Italian poet. In the *Decameron* (1349-1352), a collection of tales by Giovanni Boccaccio (1313-75), a masterpiece of classical Italian prose, Guido, while walking among the tombs in a church in Or San Michele, is mocked by his friends for brooding. He responds by saying they can mock as they will in their house—one friend realizes he means the House of Death (which Stephen, just like Guido, avoids saying). While romantic in tone and form, the *Decameron* breaks from medieval sensibility in its insistence on the human ability to overcome, even exploit, fortune.

Maiden's Rock: One of a small group of rocks near the north shore of Dalkey Island in Dublin Bay.

the basin at Clongowes. Can't see! Who's behind me?: Clongowes was the boarding school Joyce attended. There are several places in *Ulysses* where Stephen senses someone behind him, as when Bloom appears at the National Library where Stephen delivers his lecture on Shakespeare.

Lambert Simnel

Perkin Warbeck

19th-century engraving showing what Robert the Bruce might have looked like.

Their dog ambled about a bank of dwindling sand, trotting, sniffing on all sides. Looking for something lost in a past life. Suddenly he made off like a bounding hare, ears flung back, chasing the shadow of a lowskimming gull. The man's shrieked whistle struck his limp ears. He turned, bounded back, came nearer, trotted on twinkling shanks. **On a field tenney a buck, trippant, proper, unattired**. At the lacefringe of the tide he halted with stiff forehoofs, seawardpointed ears. His snout lifted barked at the wavenoise, herds of **seamorse**. They serpented towards his feet, curling, unfurling many crests, **every ninth**, breaking, plashing, from far, from farther out, waves and waves.

Cocklepickers. They waded a little way in the water and, stooping, soused their bags and, lifting them again, waded out. The dog yelped running to them, reared up and pawed them, dropping on all fours, again reared up at them with mute bearish fawning. Unheeded he kept by them as they came towards the drier sand, a rag of wolf's tongue redpanting from his jaws. His speckled body ambled ahead of them and then loped off at a calf's gallop. The carcass lay on his path. He stopped, sniffed, stalked round it, brother, nosing closer, went round it, sniffling rapidly like a dog all over the dead dog's bedraggled fell. Dogskull, dogsniff, eyes on the ground, moves to one great goal. Ah, poor dogsbody! Here lies poor dogsbody's body.

—Tatters! Out of that, you mongrel!

The cry brought him skulking back to his master and a blunt bootless kick sent him unscathed across a spit of sand, crouched in flight. He slunk back in a curve. Doesn't see me. Along by the edge of the mole he lolloped, dawdled, smelt a rock and from under a cocked hindleg pissed against it. He trotted forward and, lifting again his hindleg, pissed quick short at an unsmelt rock. The simple pleasures of the poor. His hindpaws then scattered the sand: then his forepaws dabbled and delved. **Something he buried there, his grandmother**. He rooted in the sand, dabbling, delving and stopped to listen to the air, scraped up the sand again with a fury of his claws, soon ceasing, **a pard, a panther, got in spousebreach**, vulturing the dead.

Giordano Bruno, modern portrait based on a woodcut from "Livre du recteur," 1578. Public Domain, https://commons.wikimedia.org/w/index.php?curid=52557

On a field tenney a buck, trippant, proper, unattired: Stephen translates the dog on the beach into the language of heraldry: *tenney*: orange, or tawny; *trippant*: applied to a buck or stag when passant, or walking; proper: in natural colors; *unattired*: without antlers (unusual in heraldry) because it would imply impotence). By contrast, the crest of Ireland: on a wreath *or* (gold) and *azure* (blue) a tower triple towered of the first; from the portal a *hart* (stag, buck) springing (hindlegs on ground, forelegs extended), *argent* (silver), *attired* (with antlers), and hoofed gold.

seamorse: Obsolete for walrus.

every ninth: In Irish mythology the ninth wave our from land was considered to be a magical boundary.

moves to one great goal: In Episode 2, where Stephen gets paid for his teaching and receives a lecture from the headmaster, Mr. Deasy, who proclaims "All human history moves toward one great goal, the manifestation of God." In Mr. Deasy's mouth this expresses the Victorian faith in the inevitability of man's moral and spiritual progress. By the end of the century this faith, summed up by Tennyson (1809-92), at the end of In Memorian (1850) as "one far-off divine event, / To which the whole of creation moves," was widely regarded as a feeble substitute for vital spiritual commitment. As a philosophy of history, however, it has enjoyed a rigorous heritage, from St. Augustine of Hippo (354-430) through Giordano Bruno (1548-1600), whom Joyce regarded as the "father of what is called modern philosophy," and who postulated an *anima del mondo* (Italian: "soul of the world"), as both principle and cause of nature, the indwelling presence in the light of which form and matter, being and the capacity to be, are not separable as Aristotle thought of them, but one unity. Perhaps the most significant espouser of the idea of this philosophy of history was the German philosopher Georg Wilhelm Friedrich Hegel (1770-1831), who attempted to render scientific the revealed truth of religion.

Something he buried there, his grandmother: Stephen recalls the riddle he had posed to the kids in Episode 2, the answer to which was "The fox burying his mother under a holly tree."

A pard, a panther, got in spousebreach: "spousebreach" is adultery; according to one bestiary tradition, the leopard (or panther) is born of "spousebreach" between a lioness and a pard.

Hegel, portrait by Schlesinger, 1831

Aristotle by Francesco Hayez. The Yorck Project (2002) **10.000 Meisterwerke der Malerei** *(DVD-ROM), distributed by DIRECTMEDIA Publishing GmbH. ISBN: 3936122202., Public Domain, https://commons.wikimedia.org/w/index.php?curid=152569*

After he woke me last night same dream or was it? Wait. Open hallway. Street of harlots. Remember. **Haroun al Raschid**. I am almosting it. **That man led me, spoke. I was not afraid. The melon he had he held against my face. Smiled: creamfruit smell. That was the rule, said. In. Come. Red carpet spread**. You will see who.

Shouldering their bags they trudged, **the red Egyptian**s. His blued feet out of turnedup trousers slapped the clammy sand, a dull brick muffler strangling his unshaven neck. With woman steps she followed: the ruffian and his strolling **mort**. Spoils slung at her back. Loose sand and shellgrit crusted her bare feet. About her windraw face hair trailed. Behind her lord, his helpmate, **bing awast to Romeville**. When night hides her body's flaws calling under her brown shawl from an archway where dogs have mired. Her **fancyman** is treating **two Royal Dublins in O'Loughlin's of Blackpitts. Buss** her, **wap in rogues' rum lingo**, for, **O, my dimber wapping dell! A shefiend's whiteness** under her rancid rags. **Fumbally's lane** that night: **the tanyard smells**.

White thy fambles, red thy gan
And thy quarrons dainty is.
Couch a hogshead with me then.
In the darkmans clip and kiss.

The Blackpitts section of Dublin, 1880-1900
As Stephen contemplates the gypsy couple on the sands, he imagines the woman offering herself to men in the street while her pimp works two others in a bar. Stephen is thinking of a time that he spent walking through this bleak part of town in the Liberties: In Episode 7, "Aeolus," he makes this neighborhood the fictional residence, not of the gypsy couple, but of the two women that he spotted earlier on the beach, who now star in his Parable of the Plums. Blackpitts is a short street just west of Clanbrassil Street on the south side of Dublin. Fumbally Lane runs east for a couple of blocks from the north end of Blackpitts, whose name is variously said to derive from burial pits used during plague years (the "Black Death"), or from black vats used by tanners starting in the 18th century. In 1904 this working-class neighborhood was the site not only of tanneries, but also of piggeries (pig pens) and illegal cockfighting venues. When Stephen locates his two fictional vestals in this area, saying that they "have lived fifty and fiftythree years in Fumbally's lane," Professor MacHugh asks, "Where is that?" Stephen replies, "Off Blackpitts." The thoughts of squalid sexuality that he entertained about the gypsies continue to play in his mind as he composes this scene: "Damp night reeking of hungry dough. Against the wall. Face glistening tallow under her fustian shawl. Frantic hearts. Akasic records. Quicker, darlint!" The conjunction of the two pairs of walkers in Joyce's mind may have something to do with the genesis of his heavily sexualized story, in which two aged virgins spit seeds off the top of a phallic tower.

Haroun al Rashid (763-809): caliph of Bagdad, known for the splendour of his court and for his appearance in several of the tales of the *Arabian Nights*; he supposedly disguised himself to walk unnoticed among his people.

That man led me . . . rule, said. In. Come. Red carpet spread: Stephen's dream involves the Hebraic "rule" that the first-fruits of the land were to be brought to the holy place of God's choice and there presented to the priest, whose prerequisite the first-fruits were (Deuteronomy 26:2-11). During their wanderings in the wilderness, the children of Israel complain, "our soul is dried away;" the standard gloss suggests that "the people lust for flesh," and among other fruits, they long for melons (Numbers 11:4-6) (Gifford and Seidman, *Ulysses Annotated*).

the red Egyptians: Gypsies, once thought to have been Egyptian in origin. In the passage that follows Stephen associates gypsy language with 17th-century cant, those expressions of enthusiasm for high ideals, goodness, or piety, or slang terms (*Ulysses*, Gifford/Seidman edition notes).

mort: 16th–17th-century cant (or lingo) for "woman." The word "cant" also has at its root the verb to sing, or a type of song, a canticle. A "strolling mort" in Thieves' Cant is a wandering wench who pretends to be a widow, traveling about, making laces upon staves, as Beggars tape; they are "hard-hearted, light-fingered, hypocritical and dissembling, and very dangerous to meet, if any Ruffian or Rogue be in their company." Stephen is quoting the first line of the seventh stanza of the canting song "The Rogue's Delight in Praise of his Strolling Mort." Rome means *rum*, i.e., excellent; **bing away**: "to go to." **Romeville** is the cant term for London, that is, "to go away to London" (Gifford and Seidman, *Ulysses Annotated*).

fancyman: A man who is fancied as a sweetheart; or a pimp.

Two Royal Dublins: two soldiers from the Royal Dublin Fusiliers.

O'Loughlin's of Blackpitts: Apparently a "shebeen," an unlicensed car or public house, in Blackpitts (see note in left column).

Buss (archaic) Kiss. Buss is archaic English. It is not, and never has been, cant.

wap in rogue's rum lingo: (Thieves' cant) fuck, in the excellent language of the Gypsies. The closest and obvious translation of "wap" is "fuck."

O, my dimber wapping dell: (Thieves' Cant) O, my pretty loving wench. Stephen is quoting the final stanza of the canting song.

A shefiend's whiteness: not sure about this, but I found one source that said a "shefiend" was a burlesque dancer or nocturnal creature. From another source, a "Sheffield whiteness" was classified as "white tongue," the appearance of a white coating caused by bacteria and dead cells lodged between the enlarged and sometimes inflamed papillae.

Fumbally's lane: in the Liberties in south-central Dublin.

The tanyard smells: Kelly, Dunne & Co., tanners, fellmongers, and woolmerchants, New Row South, around the corner from Fumbally's Ln. A "fellmonger" was a dealer in hides who might also prepare skins for tanning. The name is derived from the Old English 'fell' (skins) and 'monger' (dealer). Fellmongery is one of the oldest professions in the world. Today the term has become restricted to the person or the operator of the machinery which removes sheep's wool or the hair of other animals from hides in preparation for tanning. The process ohas to be done quickly after the animal is slaughtered to prevent the hides from decaying before tanning can begin (Wikipedia).

White thy fambles . . . clip and kiss: The second stanza of "The Rogue's Delight in Praise of His Strolling Mort," in Richard Head's *The Canting Academy* (1673). "fambles"—hands; "gan"—mouth; "quarrons"—body; "Couch a hogsheasd"—lie down & sleep; "darkmans"—night; other explanations of lingo appears after the poem that follows, first the 7 stanzas in 17th-century lingo, then follows translation in modernized terms.

The Rogue's Delight in Praise of His Strolling Mort

Doxy oh! Thy Glaziers shine
As Glymmar by the Salomon,
No Gentry Mort hath prats like thine
No Cove e're wap'd with such a one.

White thy fambles, red thy gan,
And thy quarrons dainty is,
Couch a hogshead with me than,
In the Darkmans clip and kiss.

What though I no Togeman wear,
Nor Commission, Mish, or slate,
Store of strummel wee'l have here.
And i'th' Skipper lib in state.

Wapping thou I know dost love,
Else the Ruffin cly thee Mort,
From thy stampers then remove
Thy Drawers and let's prig in sport.

When the Lightmans up do's call
Margery Prater from her nest,
And her Cackling cheats with all
In a Boozing-Ken wee'l feast.

There if Lour we want I'l mill
A Gage or nip for thee a bung,
Rum booz thou shalt booz thy fill
And crash a Grunting cheat that's
   young.

Bing awast to Rome-vile then
O my dimber wapping Dell,
Wee'l heave a booth and dock agen
Then trining scape and all is well.

Wench oh! Thy eyes shine
As fire by the Mass
No gentlewoman has thighs like thine
No fellow ever made love with such a
one.

White thy hands, red thy mouth,
And thy body dainty is,
Lie down with me then,
In the night embrace and kiss.

What though I no cloak wear,
Nor shirt, chemise, or sheet,
Plenty of straw we'll have here.
And in the barn sleep in state.

Copulating thou I know dost love,
Else the Devil seize thee, wench,
From thy feet then remove
Thy stockings and let's ride in sport.

When the Sun rises and does call
The hen from her nest,
And her chickens withal
In a tippling-house we'll feast.

There if money we want I'll steal
A pot or nab for thee a purse,
Excellent liquor thou shalt drink thy fill
And crunch a pig that's young.

Go away to London then
O my pretty loving wench,
We'll rob a house and fuck again,
Then hanging escape and all is well.

While the word "dock" in the final verse is actually an intentional euphemism since in this instance the word wap (or fuck), would be without poetic force. Stephen translates the Shakespearean term "buss" into cant. On the term "lingo," Eric Partridge writes:

> *"Lingo was in [the 18th century], and occ[asionally] later, a synonym of the slang, the flash (language); just—only just—possibly it was, for a decade, c[ant] in this specific sense."*

Fumbally Lane is a narrow and historic street in Dublin, Ireland, south of the city centre in The Liberties. In name and character it is perhaps the most evocative of all the Liberties' streets. It connects Blackpitts to New Street and is close to St Patrick's Cathedral.

This area was originally part of the Liberty of Thomas Court and Donore (later called the Earl of Meath's Liberty), having been granted by Henry VIII to Sir William Brabazon, whose ancestors became the Earls of Meath after the dissolution of the monasteries in 1538. This location was then on the fringes of the expanding 18th-century city when the lane itself was set out by local brewer and Quaker Jacob Poole in 1721 to connect Blackpitts (where he had property) to New Street The lane has long had mixed industrial and residential use. Historically, tanning, brewing and associated industries flourished in this part of Dublin, partly because the River Poddle is close by. The industrial heritage of the area even dates back even to the mid-17th century and is linked to and influenced by both Quakers and Huguenots. In 2006 archaeologists found evidence of medieval leather tanning off Fumbally Lane and nearby New Street with wood-lined soaking pits and elaborate ditch systems. They also identified that one of the existing large old former brewery buildings on Fumbally dates from the 1740s.

Brewing flourished in the area since the mid-1700s. It is possible that the first Dublin porter was brewed here. The Poole and Taylor families, who were related, had brewing interests here from at least that time and before. In 1779 Samuel Madder operated the Blackpitts Porter Company and acquired a brewery. In 1830 John Busby acquired a brewery property in Fumbally and erected a new distillery here. A building features his initials and the year 1836 on a 'cast iron water tank'. This particular refurbished 19th-century stone-faced building is part of the Fumbally Studio development and now home to both apartments and an office building.

The name Fumbally is a peculiar one and one that provokes a wide range of theories and suggestions as to its origin. The street is officially called Fumbally Lane or Lána Fumbally. It has had many name variations since 1721. The lane first appears in a 1728 map without a name and with variations in subsequent maps as 'Bumbailiff's Lane' and 'Fumbailie's Lane'. It is mistakenly suggested by Rev. McCready in Dublin Street Names: Dated and Explained that Fumbally's Lane (as it was then referred to in Thom's Directory) was just a 'corruption of Bumbailiff's-lane'. [8] Fumbally's Lane is also the name James Joyce uses in Chapter 3 of *Ulysses* where he refers to "the tanyard smells."

However, there is some evidence that the name derives from a local Huguenot family named Fontvielle, Fomboilie, Fombily, Fombela, Fonveille, or Fombally. Christine Casey refers to the street association with a Huguenot family called Fombily; supporting this, Peter Pearson provides two names—David Fombily and Anthony Fombily—who were described as 'skinners.' There is further evidence from Registry of Deeds entry of an assignment mentioned in 1893 and a reference written in 1915 refers to a Royal Dublin Society prize for life drawing in March 1746 won by a 'Mr. Fombally'; these all suggest that a Fombally or Fombely family resided in Dublin and were associated with this lane in the mid-18th century. In addition, records retrieved from the International Genealogical Index show a half-dozen Fonvielles all born or christened in Dublin at Peter St. Church and at Lucy Lane at the beginning of the 18th Century (Wikipedia).

Morose delectation Aquinas tunbelly calls this, *frate porcospino.* **Unfallen Adam rode and not rutted.** Call away let him: *thy quarrons dainty is.* Language no whit worse than his. Monkwords, **marybeads** jabber on their girdles: rogueworks, tough nuggets patter in their pockets.

Passing now.

A side eye at my **Hamlet hat.** If I were suddenly naked here as I sit? I am not. **Across the sands of all the world, followed by the sun's flaming sword, to the west, trekking to evening lands. She trudges, schlepps, trains, drags, trascines her load.** A tide westering, moondrawn, in her wake. Tides, myriadislanded, within her, blood not mine, *oinopa ponton,* a winedark sea. **Behold the handmaid of the moon.** In sleep the wet sign calls her hour, bids her rise. Bridebed, childbed, bed of death, ghostcandled. **Omnis caro ad te veniet. He comes, pale vampire, through storm his eyes, his bat sails bloodying the sea, mouth to her mouth's kiss.**

Here. Put a pin in that chap, will you? **My tablets.** Mouth to her kiss. No. Must be two of em. Glue em well. Mouth to her mouth's kiss.

Cockle hat and staff

Harun al-Rashid as depicted in **The Arabian Nights**

Rear of houses in Blckpitts, 1913

Morose delectation: Thomas Aquinas in *Summa Theologica: delectatio morosa*, an internal sin, taking pleasure in sinful thoughts.

tunbelly: Because the St. Thomas of medieval legend was so big-bellied that tables had to be cut out to fit around his stomach.

frate porcospino: Italian: "the porcupine monk" or "Brother Porcupine;" that is, Aquinas's argument is prickly and difficult to attack.

Unfallen Adam . . . not rutted: According to tradition, before the Fall, sexual intercourse was without lust.

marybeads: the beads of their rosaries, since the rosary includes a cycle of fifteen Hail Marys among its prayers.

my Hamlet hat: In *Hamlet*, Ophelia sings that she'll know her true love by his "cockle hat and staff and his sandal shoon" (Hamlet IV.v.23-26). The cockle hat has a scallop shell as a sign of pilgrimage, especially to the shrine of St. James of Compostela in Spain.

Across the sands . . . evening lands: Joyce is probably alluding to *Hellas* (1821), a verse drama by Percy Bysshe Shelley (1792-1822), written while he was living in Pisa, with a view to raising money for the Greek War of Independence, which began in March of 1821 and in which Shelley saw the dawn of a new Golden Age. It was to be Shelley's last published poem during his lifetime. The last chorus from the drama contains the much-quoted stanzas:

> The world's great age begins anew,
>   The golden years return,
> The earth doth like a snake renew
>   Her winter weeds outworn:
> Heaven smiles, and faiths and empires gleam,
> Like wrecks of a dissolving dream.

Stephen may also be referring to the flaming sword, "which turned every which way, to keep the way of the tree of life" that God placed outside the Garden of Eden after evicting Adam and Eve (Gen.3:24)

She trudges, schlepps, trains, drags, trascines her load: "She" is Eve (Gen.3:16); the verbs are all synonyms with different linguistic origins: English (Anglo-Saxon root), Yiddish, French, English (Anglo-Saxon root), and Italian. Her load of "sorrow" was "greatly multiplied" by the Fall.

oinopa ponton: Homeric Greek, the "wine-dark sea," which first occurs in Book One of the *Odyssey* and recurs throughout. Buck Mulligan invokes the epithet while shaving atop the Martello Tower in Episode 1.

Behold the handmaid of the moon: ss Luke I:38: "Behold the handmaid [Mary] of the Lord."

Omnis caro ad te veniet: Latin: "All flesh will come to thee," from Psalms 65:2: "O thou that hearest prayer, unto thee shall all flesh come"; part of the Introit (the entrance chant) of the requiem mass.

He comes . . . mouth's kiss: Stephen's "poem" is a freely borrowed, free adaptation of "My Grief on the Sea," a Gaelic poem from *Love Songs of Connacht* translated by Douglas Hyde, Irish literary nationalist, poet, scholar, friend of Yeats, and president of Ireland (1938-45). The vision of the pale vampire points forward to the encounter with Leopold Bloom, as well as to the dream Stephen had the previous night, a "street of harlots," which suggests the climactic "Circe" episode at Bella Cohen's brothel in Nighttown.

My tablets: Hamlet, momentarily deranged by the psychological impact of the Ghost and its message, writes an aphorism about villainy and his uncle in his notebook: "My tablets—meet it is I set it down." (I.v.107)

His lips lipped and mouthed fleshless lips of air: mouth to her moomb. Oomb, allwombing tomb. His mouth moulded issuing breath, unspeeched: ooeeehah: roar of cataractic planets, globed, blazing, roaring wayawayawayawayaway. Paper. The banknotes, blast them. Old Deasy's letter. Here. Thanking you for the hospitality tear the blank end off. Turning his back to the sun he bent over far to a table of rock and **scribbled words**. That's twice I forgot to take slips from the library counter.

His shadow lay over the rocks as he bent, ending. Why not endless till the farthest star? Darkly they are there behind this light, **darkness shining in the brightness, delta of Cassiopeia**, worlds. Me sits there with his **augur's rod of ash**, in borrowed sandals, by day beside a livid sea, unbeheld, in violet night walking beneath a reign of uncouth stars. I throw this ended shadow from me, manshape ineluctable, call it back. Endless, would it be mine, **form of my form**? Who watches me here? **Who ever anywhere will read these written words?** Signs on a white field. Somewhere to someone in your flutiest voice. **The good bishop of Cloyne** took **the veil of the temple** out of **his shovel hat**: veil of space with coloured emblems hatched on its field. Hold hard. Coloured on a flat: yes, that's right. Flat I see, then think distance, near, far, flat I see, east, back. Ah, see now! Falls back suddenly, frozen in stereoscope. Click does the trick. You find my words dark. Darkness is in our souls do you not think? Flutier. Our souls, shamewounded by our sins, cling to us yet more, a woman to her lover clinging, the more the more.

James Joyce

James Joyce

William Alexander, Archbishop of Armagh, caricatured in 1895, wearing a bishop's apron, gaiters, and low-crowned shovel hat.

darkness shining in the brightness: After John 1:4-5. This is the second time Stephen refers to this quote; the first was in the previous episode: "In [God] was life; and the life was the light of men. And the light shineth in the darkness; and the darkness comprehended it not." **delta of Cassiopeia**: Delta is a relatively inconspicuous star (of the third magnitude) in the constellation of Cassiopeia, a W in the northern skies. Delta is at the bottom of the left-hand loop of the W. In Episode 9, in his lecture on Shakespeare at the National Library, Stephen alludes to this star as a "daystar, eastward of the bear." The Danish astronomer Tycho Brahe (1546-1601) discovered a super-nova above the small start in the W-shaped constellation on November 11, 1572 (Shakespeare was eight-and-a-half years old). The nova, called Tycho's Star, brightened rapidly until it outshone all the other stars and planets at night and was visible in the daylight. It lasted for sixteen months, causing enough imaginative excitement in Elizabethan England as a star of Bethlehem, that many felt it heralded a new birth, the second coming of Christ. **augur's rod of ash**: The Roman augur's rod, the lituus, was used to note omens given by birds. See note on Stephen's "ash-sword," or ash-plant at the beginning of "Proteus" on 60 of this publication. **form of my form**: Arisitotle; see note on 59.

Who ever anywhere will read these written words?: The irony is not lost that Stephen is referring to the poem he just scribbled on the piece of paper torn from Deasy's letter, but we can also hear Joyce asking the same question of his book. Later, in Episode 13, "Nausica," when Bloom is out walking on the Sandymount, he finds something: "Mr. Bloom stopped and turned over a piece of paper on the strand. He brought it near his eyes and peered. Letter? No. Can't read. Better go. Better. I'm tired to move. Page of an old copybook. Never know what you find. Children always want to throw things in the sea."

the good bishop of Cloyne: George Berkeley (1685-1753) was one of the great philosophers of the early modern period. He was a brilliant critic of his predecessors, particularly Descartes, Malebranche, and Locke. He was a talented metaphysician famous for defending idealism, that is, the view that reality consists exclusively of minds and their ideas. His most-studied works, the *Treatise Concerning the Principles of Human Knowledge* (when I studied him in college, my professor referred to the famous essay as the Principles, for short) and *Three Dialogues between Hylas and Philonous* (which my professor referred to as simply the *Dialogues*, not to be confused, of course, with Plato's), are beautifully written and dense with the sort of arguments that delight contemporary philosophers. He was also a wide-ranging thinker with interests in religion (which were fundamental to his philosophical motivations), the psychology of vision, mathematics, physics, morals, economics, and medicine. Although many of Berkeley's first readers greeted him with incomprehension, he influenced both Hume and Kant, and is much read (if little followed) in our own day (www.cloyne.ie).

the veil of the temple . . . frozen in stereoscope: Berkeley argued that reality itself is mental—things do not exist, ideas alone exist—so he found reality inside his own head. The "veil of the temple" (Exodus 26:31-5) separates the "holy place" from the "most holy place," (behind the veil), with the veil acting as a multicolored screen. And the veil is rent at the moment of Jesus's death (Matthew 27:51). This is perhaps an indication that Berkeley goes beyond idealist philosophy to super-idealism in making all reality mental. The rest of the passage follows Berkeley's experiments with vision in his *Essay Towards as New Theory of Vision* (1709), claiming that "Vision is the Language of the Author of Nature." Berkeley maintains that we can't see ". . . the images of anything without the mind," that what we see we see as flat distance is thought not seen; the veil, like a screen, is like the visible world upon which God projects signs (or ideas) to be *read* and *thought*, rather than *seen*. In other words, we think them into "stereoscope." Thus, the signs on the screen could be regarded as something taken out of one's head (or hat).

Notes continued on 115

She trusts me, her hand gentle, the longlashed eyes. Now where the blue hell am I bringing her beyond the veil? Into **the ineluctable modality of the ineluctable visuality**. She, she, she. What she? The virgin at **Hodges Figgis' window** on Monday looking in for one of **the alphabet books** you were going to write. Keen glance you gave her. Wrist through the braided jess of her sunshade. She lives in **Leeson park** with a grief and kickshaws, a lady of letters. Talk that to someone else, **Stevie: a pickmeup**. Bet she wears **those curse of God stays suspenders** and yellow stockings, darned with lumpy wool. Talk about apple dumplings, **piuttosto**. Where are your wits?

Touch me. Soft eyes. Soft soft soft hand. I am lonely here. **O, touch me** soon, now. **What is that word known to all men?** I am quiet here alone. Sad too. Touch, touch me.

Hodges Figgis,
present day

"Those curse of God
stays suspenders and
yellow stockings talk
about apple dumplings."

A shovel hat: worn by some Church of Ireland and Church of England clergy, particularly arch-deacons and bishops in the eighteenth century. The hat was usually made of black beaver or felt, and had a low, round crown and a wide brim, which projected in a shovel-like curve at the front and rear and was often worn turned up at the sides. Like the tricorne it was a development of the low-crowned broad-brimmed hats fashionable in the later 17th century. Along with the bishop's apron and gaiters, the shovel hat was an instantly recognizable accoutrement of senior Anglican clergy between the 18th and late 19th century, although it was also worn by parsons and less senior figures. By the mid 19th century it was already seen as somewhat traditionalist or old-fashioned: Thomas Carlyle coined the term "shovelhattery" to attack hidebound orthodoxy in the Church of England. The term "broad-brimmed," occasionally used to describe Anglican churchmen in the 19th century (particularly the Evangelical party) was also derived from the shovel hat (Wikipedia).

The ineluctable modality . . . visuality: see note on 59.

Hodges Figgis' window: booksellers and publishers founded 1768, 104 Grafton Street, between Trinity College and St. Stephen's Green.

Lesson Park: a street (and the local name for the area) south of the Grand Canal on the then-sur-burban outskirts of metropolitan Dublin.

Talk that to someone else, Stevie: a pickmeup: Echoes Stephen's friend Davin, whose notable experience with a pick up is recalled by Stephen in *A Portrait of the Artist*. Davin addresses Stephen as Stevie, "the homely version of his Christian name."

those curse of God stays suspenders: A corset with garters; "curse of God" because it functioned as a chastity belt.

Piuttosto: Italian: "rather."

What is that word known to all men?: Stephen returns to this question in Episode 9, "Scylla and Charybdis," and in Episode 15, "Circe," where he says, "Tell me the word, mother, if you know now. The word known to all men." Stephen seems to regard the question as a mystery. The key to the mystery seems to be not the word itself but the word-made-manifest. But in the first edition of *Ulysses*, and in all subsequent editions during Joyce's lifetime, not to mention the revised Random House 1961 edition, the answer to the question is never given. But in one of the galley drafts, known as the *Rosenbach Manuscript* (which was sold to John Quinn, a New York lawyer who later auctioned it off to Rosenbach), Joyce provides the answer, which he later deleted. In "Scylla and Charybdis," he says during his lecture on Shakespeare: "Love, yes. Word known to all men." The 1984 *Ulysses* (the Gabler version, hotly controversial) reinstates the phrase in that episode. Bloom also alludes to love as being the cornerstone of life in Episode 12, "Cyclops," when he refers to Jesus's words in the New Testament. I doubt that Joyce would have approved of Gabler's rein-statement of the word since I believe Joyce felt that only in the experience of love can the word known to all men be truly *known*. Of all the criticisms Gabler received for his 1984 "Corrected Text," this amendation drew the most fire. For more on this controversy, see the essay at the end of these notes, "What Is the Word Known to All Men?"

He lay back at full stretch over the sharp rocks, cramming the scribbled note and pencil into a pock his hat. His hat down on his eyes. That is Kevin Egan's movement I made, nodding for his nap, sabbath sleep. *Et vidit Deus. Et erant valde bona. Alo! Bonjour.* **Welcome as the flowers in May. Under its leaf he watched through peacocktwittering lashes the southing sun. I am caught in this burning scene. Pan's hour, the faunal noon. Among gumheavy serpentplants, milkoozing fruits, where on the tawny waters leaves lie wide. Pain is far.**

The Afternoon of a Faun
(Stéphane Mallarmé)

These nymphs, I would perpetuate them.
So bright
Their crimson flesh that hovers there, light
In the air drowsy with dense slumbers.
Did I love a dream?
My doubt, mass of ancient night, ends
    extreme
In many a subtle branch, that remaining the
    true
Woods themselves, proves, alas, that I too
Offered myself, alone, as triumph,
the false ideal of roses.

Inert, all things burn in the tawny hour
Not seeing by what art there fled away
    together
Too much of hymen desired by one who
    seeks there
The natural A: then I'll wake to the primal
    fever
Erect, alone, beneath the ancient flood, light's
    power,
Lily! And the one among you all for
    artlessness.

Other than this sweet nothing shown by their
    lip, the kiss
That softly gives assurance of treachery,
My breast, virgin of proof, reveals the
    mystery
Of the bite from some illustrious tooth
    planted;
Let that go! Such the arcane chose for
    confidant,
The great twin reed we play under the azure
    ceiling,
That turning towards itself the cheek's
    quivering,

Dreams, in a long solo, so we might amuse
The beauties round about by false notes that
    confuse
Between itself and our credulous singing;
And create as far as love can, modulating,
The vanishing, from the common dream of
    pure flank
Or back followed by my shuttered glances,
Of a sonorous, empty and monotonous line.

I hold the queen!
O certain punishment…
No, but the soul
Void of words, and this heavy body,
Succumb to noon's proud silence slowly:
With no more ado, forgetting blasphemy, I
Must sleep, lying on the thirsty sand, and as I
Love, open my mouth to wine's true
    constellation!

Farewell to you, both: I go to see the shadow
    you have become

Mallarmé as a faun, cover of the literary magazine Les hommes d'aujourd'hui, *1887*

---

sabbath sleep, *Et vidit . . . bona*: Latin: (from Genesis I:31) "And God saw [everything that he had made,] and, [behold], it was very good."

Welcome as the flowers in May: from the song "You're as Welcome as the Flowers in May," by Dan J. Sullivan.

Under its leaf . . . Pain is far: an improvisation on Stéphen Mallarmé's (1842-98) "L'Après-midi d'un faune" (1876). Noon is both Pan's hour (the Greek nature god's most active time) and the hour of Proteus's downfall (the time when, readying himself for sleep, he is caught by Menelasus). Mallarmé's poem describes the sensual experiences of a faun who has just woken up from his afternoon sleep and discusses his encounters with several nymphs during the morning in a dreamlike monologue. It is Mallarmé's best-known work and a hallmark in the history of symbolism in French literature. Paul Valéry considered it to be the greatest poem in French literature. For the publication, Mallarmé's long-time friend Édouard Manet created four wood-engraved embellishments which were printed in black, and hand-tinted in pink by Manet himself in order to save money. Mallarmé's poem would provide the inspiration for many musical works, the most prominent of which being *Prélude à L'après-midi d'un Faune* by Claude Debussy. Other composers who drew subject matter and inspiration from Mallarmé's poetry include Maurice Ravel in *Trois poèmes de Mallarmé* (1913), Darius Milhaud with *Chansons bas de Stéphane Mallarmé* (1917), and Pierre Boulez, with his hour-long solo soprano and orchestra piece *Pli selon pli* (1957–62). The poem also served basis for the ballets *Afternoon of a Faun* by Vaslav Nijinsky (1912), Jerome Robbins (1953) and Tim Rushton (2006). Debussy's orchestral work and Nijinsky's ballet would be of great significance in the development of modernism in the arts (Wikipedia).

Stéphane Mallarmé was recognized as one of France's four major poets of the second half of the 19th Century, along with Charles Baudelaire, Paul Verlaine, and Arthur Rimbaud. Much of his poetry was acknowledged to be difficult to understand because of its tortuous syntax, ambiguous expressions, and obscure imagery. His poetry became highly influential in France and beyond, including in the United States, among poets looking for new and innovative ways to write, during the turbulent times of the early 1900s. After an undistinguished school career, he took a teaching post in the small town of Tournon just south of Lyon. He was to remain a teacher, although a reluctant and not very good one. After several unsuccessful attempts, he managed to obtain early retirement on health grounds in November 1893. By then his reputation as France's greatest living poet was firmly established through the publication of his poems in various literary magazines and partial collections and through the admiring essay on him that Verlaine wrote in his celebrated volume *Les Poètes Maudits* (The Accursed Poets, 1884). The "mardis," weekly Tuesday evening meetings that he held in his Paris apartment from 1880 onward, were eagerly attended by the leading figures in literature, painting, and music. His retirement meant that he was able to spend more time at his country retreat at Valvins on the banks of the upper Seine, where he died unexpectedly on September 9, 1898 at the age of 56. The relatively small number of poems Mallarmé wished to preserve—some 50 in all—were collected in one slim volume of *Les Poésies de S. Mallarmé,* which appeared early in 1899. Near the end of his life he wrote a work that deserves particular mention because of its extreme originality and the notoriety it has achieved: *Un coup de dés jamais n'abolira le hasard* (A throw of the dice will never abolish chance, 1914), which originally appeared in the May 1897 issue of *Cosmopolis* (poetryfoundation.org).

And no more turn aside and brood.

His gaze brooded on his broadtoed boots, a buck's castoffs, *nebeneinander*. He counted the creases of rucked leather wherein another's foot had nested warm. The foot that beat the ground in **tripudium**, foot I dislove. But you were delighted when Esther Osvalt's shoe went on you: girl I knew in Paris. *Tiens, quel petit pied!* Staunch friend, a brother soul: **Wilde's love that dare not speak its name**. His arm: Cranly's arm. He now will leave me. And the blame? As I am. As I am. **All or not at all.**

In long lassoes from the **Cock lake** the water flowed full, covering greengoldenly lagoons of sand, rising, flowing. My ashplant will float away. I shall wait. No, they will pass on, passing, chafing against the low rocks, swirling, passing. Better get this job over quick. Listen: a fourworded wavespeech: seesoo, hrss, rsseeiss, ooos. Vehement breath of waters amid seasnakes, rearing horses, rocks. In cups of rocks it slops: flop, slop, slap: bounded in barrels. And, spent, its speech ceases. It flows purling, widely flowing, floating foampool, flower unfurling.

Under the upswelling tide he saw the writhing weeds lift languidly and sway reluctant arms, hising up their petticoats, in whispering water swaying and upturning coy silver fronds. Day by day: night by night: lifted, flooded and let fall. Lord, they are weary; and, whispered to, they sigh.

***

Joyce Reviews Ibsen, Ibsen Replies, Joyce Replies

When Joyce was 18, his positive review of Ibsen's play *When We Dead Awaken* was published in the *Fortnightly Review*, quite a prestigious journal. Ibsen's translator, William Archer, showed him the review and Ibsen contacted Archer, telling him to let Joyce know how much he had appreciated it. Joyce wrote Archer the following response:

"Dear Sir: I wish to thank you for your kindness in writing to me. I am a young Irishman, eighteen years old, and the words of Ibsen I shall keep in my heart all my life." A year later Joyce wrote to Ibsen on the occasion of his 73rd birthday: "When you were an undergraduate at the University as I am, and if you think what it would have meant to you to have earned a word from one who held as high a place in your esteem as you hold in mine, you will understand my feeling. Do not think me a hero-worshipper—I am not so. And when I spoke of you in debating societies and so forth, I enforced attention by no futile ranting. But we always keep the dearest things to ourselves. I did not tell them what bound me closest to you. I did not say how what I could discern dimly of your life was my pride to see, how your battles inspired me—not the obvious material battles but those that were fought and won behind your forehead, how your willful resolution to wrest the secret from life gave me heart and how in your absolute indifference to public canons of art, friends and shibboleths you walked in the light of your inward heroism. And this is what I write to you of now." He concludes his letter with these words: "As one of the young generation for whom you have spoken I give you greeting—not humbly, because I am obscure and you in the glare, not sadly, because you are an old man and I a young man, not presumptuously, not sentimentally—but joyfully, with hope and with love, I give you greeting." *When We Dead*

(Continued on bottom of next page)

And no more turn aside and brood: from W. B. Yeats's poem "Who Goes with Fergus?" which was included as a song in the first version of his play, *The Countess Cathleen* (1892). The song is sung to comfort the countess, who has sold her soul to the powers of darkness so that her people might have food. In the poem, Fergus represents the archetype of the mystical poet who gives up the pursuit of the worldly to seek spiritual realms.

Who will go drive with Fergus now,
And pierce the deep wood's woven shade,
And dance upon the level shore?
Young man, lift up your russet brow,
And lift your tender eyelids, maid,
And brood on hopes and fear no more.

And no more turn aside and brood
Upon love's bitter mystery;
For Fergus rules the brazen cars,
And rules the shadows of the wood,
And the white breast of the dim sea
And all dishevelled wandering stars.

nebeneinander: things proximate in space; see note on 61.

tripudium: Latin: literally, "a triple beat or stroke;" figuratively, "a measured stamping, leaping, jumping, dancing;" in ritual, "a solemn religious dance."

Tiens, quel petit pied!: French, "My, what a small foot!"

Wilde's love that dare not speak its name: the phrase appears in "Two Loves," a poem by Lord Alfred Douglas (1870-1945), friend of Oscar Wilde:

I am true love, I fill
The hearts of boy and girl with mutual flame.
Then sighing said the other, "Have thy will,
I am the love that dare not speak its name.

In 1895, Wilde brought a libel action against the eighth marquess of Queensbury, Lord Alfred Douglas's father, claiming that the marquess had accused him of homosexual practices. Wilde lost the libel suit. He was then arrested and tried for "indecency and sodomy." Wilde declared that "The 'Love that dare not speak its name' in this century is such a great affection of an elder for a younger man as there was between David and Jonathan. It is that deep, spiritual affection that is pure as it is perfect." He was convicted and sentenced to two years in prison.

All or not at all: in Henrik Ibsen's *Brand* (1866), Brand announces, "My claim is 'nought or all.'" Brand refuses to visit and absolve his dying mother, just as Stephen has refused to pray at his mother's deathbed in the interim between *A Portrait of the Artist* and *Ulysses*.

Cock lake: a tidal pool off Sandymount.

(Joyce Reviews Ibsen continued from previous page)

Awaken was Ibsen's last and shortest play. It was not particularly well received, and it has rarely been performed. His English translator was disappointed with it and wrote the following in *The Collected Works of Henrik Ibsen*, published in 1911: "To pretend to rank it with his masterpieces is to show a very imperfect sense of the nature of their mastery." Joyce could discern what the critics were unable to see. As Mimmi Beck wrote in her article "Symbolism overshadows *When We Dead Awaken*," published in the Feb. 26, 1991, issue of *The Tech*, the play wasn't for everyone: "Overall, *When We Dead Awaken* is a complex play about art and love that demands an audience willing to work to figure out its tantalizing symbolism, willing to be bombarded with irritating sounds and willing to fill slow moments with their own thoughts about the issues. It is a play that will either leave you frustrated, or up for hours of discussion." Joyce was up for complex writing filled with tantalizing symbolism, and if there were discussions to be had, he would be willing to spend hours entertaining the issues.

Saint Ambrose heard it, sigh of leaves and waves, waiting, awaiting the fullness of their times, *diebus ac noctibus iniurias patiens ingemiscit*. To no end gathered; vainly then released, forthflowing, wending back: loom of the moon. Weary too in sight of lovers, lascivious men, **a naked woman shining in her courts**, she draws a toil of waters.

Five fathoms out there. **Full fathom five thy father lies**. At one, he said. Found drowned. High water at Dublin bar. Driving before it a loose drift of rubble, fanshoals of fishes, silly shells. A corpse rising saltwhite from the undertow, bobbing **a pace a pace a porpoise** landward. There he is. Hook it quick. Pull. **Sunk though he be beneath the watery floor**. We have him. Easy now.

***

John Milton: *Lycidas*

Herodotus in his *Histories*, Book IX (written in the 5th century BCE) mentions an Athenian councilor in Salamis, "a man named Lycidas" who proposed to his fellow citizens that they submit to a compromise offered by their enemy, Persian King Xerxes I, with whom they were at war. Suspected of collusion with the enemy for suggesting the compromise, Lycidas was stoned to death by "those in the council and those outside, [who] were so enraged . . . . With all the uproar in Salamis over Lycidas, the Athenian women soon found out what had happened; whereupon, without a word from the men, they got together, and, each one urging on her neighbor and taking her along with the crowd, flocked to Lycidas' house and stoned his wife and children." The name later occurs in Theocritus's Idylls (3rd century BC), where Lycidas is most prominently a poet-goatherd. The name appears several times in Virgil (70-19 BC) and is a typically Doric shepherd's name, appropriate for the pastoral mode. A Lycidas appears in Ovid's (late 1st century BC – early 1st century A.D.) Metamorphoses as a centaur. Lycidas also occurs in Lucan's Pharsalia, where in iii.636 a sailor named Lycidas is ripped by an iron hook from the deck of a ship. By naming Edward King "Lycidas," Milton follows the tradition of memorializing a loved one through Pastoral poetry, a practice that may be traced from ancient Greek Sicily through Roman culture and into the Christian Middle Ages and early Renaissance. Milton describes King as "selfless," even though he was of the clergy—a statement both bold and, at the time, controversial among lay people: "Through allegory, the speaker accuses God of unjustly punishing the young, selfless King, whose premature death ended a career that would have unfolded in stark contrast to the majority of the ministers and bishops of the Church of England, whom the speaker condemns as depraved, materialistic, and selfish."

Renaissance writers used the pastoral mode in order to represent an ideal of life in a simple, rural landscape. Literary critics have emphasized the artificial character of pastoral nature: The pastoral was in its very origin a sort of toy, literature of make-believe. Milton himself recognized the pastoral as one of the natural modes of literary expression, employing it throughout Lycidas in order to achieve a strange juxtaposition between death and the remembrance of a loved one.

The poem was exceedingly popular. It was hailed as Milton's best poem, and by some as the greatest lyrical poem in the English language. Yet it was detested for its artificiality by Samuel Johnson, who found "the diction is harsh, the rhymes uncertain, and the numbers unpleasing" and complained that "in this poem there is no nature, for there is no truth; there is no art, for there is nothing new." It is from a line in Lycidas that Thomas Wolfe took the name of his novel *Look Homeward, Angel*:

Look homeward Angel now, and melt with ruth:
And, O ye Dolphins, waft the hapless youth.

(Wikipedia)

Saint Ambrose; *diebus ac noctibus . . . ingemiscit*: Ambrose (340-97), Bishop of Milan, one of the four Doctors of the Western Church (along with St. Augustine, Jerome, and Gregory the Great), in his *Commentary on Romans*: Latin: "Days and nights [the Creation] groans over wrongs" (on Romans, 8:22). Of the Eastern Church, the four Doctors were St. Athanasius, Basil the Great, Gregory Nazianzen, and John Chrysostum.

a naked woman shining in her courts: John Dryden (1631-1700) in *Mac Flecknoe* (1682) describes the "brothel houses" of the Barbican in London: Scenes of lewd loves, and of polluted joys / Where their vast courts the mother-strumpers keep, / And, undisturbed by watch, in silence sleep." Dryden himself is parodying two lines from Abraham Cowley's (1618-67) unfinished biblical epic *Davideis* (1656): Where their vast Courts the Mother-Waters keep, / And undisturb'd by Moon in Silence sleep."

Full fathom five thy father lies: opening of Ariel's song in *The Tempest*, Act I, scene 2.

> Full fathom five thy father lies;
> Of his bones are coral made;
> Those are pearls that were his eyes:
> Nothing of him that doth fade
> But doth suffer a seachange,
> Sea-nymphs hourly ring his knell:
> Ding-dong
> Hark! Now I hear them—Ding dong bell.

(In T.S. Eliot's *The Waste Land* (1922), Eliot quotes the lines: "Those were pearls that were his eyes.")

a pace a pace a porpoise: This sounds suspiciously like an allusion or part of a nursery rhyme. One possibility is in Milton's *Paradise Lost*, as Sin and her son Death approach Earth after the Fall: "behind her [Sin] Death / Close following pace for pace, not mounted yet / On his pale horse" (10:588-90).

Sunk though he be beneath the watery floor: Line 167 of Milton's (1608-74) *Lycidas* (1638), pastoral elegy on the death of his friend Edward King, who drowned when his ship sank in the Irish Sea off the coast of Wales in August 1637.

> Weep no more, woeful Shepherds weep no more,
> For Lycidas your sorrow is not dead,
> Sunk though he be beneath the wat'ry floor,
> So sinks the day-star in the Ocean bed,
> And yet anon repairs his drooping head,
> And tricks his beams, and with new spangled Ore,
> Flames in the forehead of the morning sky:
> So Lycidas, sunk low, but mounted high,
> Through the dear might of him that walk'd the waves,
> Where other groves, and other streams along,
> With Nectar pure his oozy Locks he laves,
> And hears the unexpressive nuptial Song,
> In the blest Kingdom meek of joy and love.

Bag of corpsegas sopping in foul brine. A quiver of minnows, fat of a spongy titbit, flash through the slits of his buttoned trouserfly. **God becomes man becomes fish becomes barnacle goose becomes featherbed mountain**. Dead breaths I living breathe, tread dead dust, devour a urinous offal from all dead. Hauled stark over the gunwale he breathes upward the stench of his green grave, his leprous nosehole snoring to the sun.

A seachange this, brown eyes saltblue. **Seadeath**, mildest of all deaths known to man. **Old Father Ocean**. *Prix de Paris*: **beware of imitations**. Just you **give it a fair trial**. We enjoyed ourselves immensely.

Old Father

Stephen thinks briefly of his quest for spiritual fatherhood—his reference to "Old Father Ocean" touching upon the Father-Son theme which will play out in the penultimate episode when Bloom rescues Stephen from the bullying sailors at Bella Cohen's brothel and takes him home to sober him up. It is the only reference Joyce makes in this episode to the Homeric epithet halios gerôn, sometimes rendered as the Old Man of the Sea. The entwining of Shakespearean and Homeric parallels continues in this episode as Stephen turns from The Tempest's mystical consolation for a death by drowning ("Full fathom five thy father lies . . . A seachange this") to the *Odyssey's* benign prophecy that its hero will die at sea ("Seadeath, mildest of all deaths known to man"). Stephen associates this death with "Old Father Ocean," Proteus. Stephen is terrified of water, but having just thought of the drowned man undergoing a sequence of benign metamorphoses ("God becomes man becomes fish becomes barnacle goose becomes featherbed mountain"), he entertains Tiresias' words calmly. The central concern in this episode has been protean flux: the distressing impermanence of all earthly things, against which the human mind wages perpetual war. Thus Joyce not only renders this concern through narrative action and interior monologue, but through the technique of "stream of consciousness" (pun intended on "protean ocean").

But by far the most powerfully suggestive analogue to Homer's story lies in Stephen's restless, relentless meditations on change. Everything around him is in flux: the incoming tide, rotting and rusting objects, burping sewage gases, people and animals and ships and breezes passing by. Language, his medium for contemplating the world, is constantly shifting as English gives way to French, Latin, Italian, German, Irish, Scottish, Spanish, Greek, Hebrew, and 17th century gypsy "cant." Memories take him to Paris, the slums of Dublin, his aunt's house, Clongowes Wood College, the Howth tram, the Sandycove tower, churches, a library, a bookstore. Imagination takes him to scenes of starvation, war, exile, and political intrigue. Stephen replays past follies and pretensions, obsessions and temptations. His mother's death was only one of many kinds of dying: death is everywhere for him: the shells that crunch underfoot housed former sea creatures; seaweed that holds the rotting body of a dog; ocean waves depositing the corpse of a drowned man; the wreckage of the Spanish Armada and members of the crew dying in their watery grave; whales stranded on the beach, Viking rampages, a murdered post office worker; even the dead fetus carried in the midwife's bag; even a buried mother.

As Menalaus wrestles Proteus to find out the future, Stephen is wrestling with himself, struggling to find answers. Stephen admits at the opening of the episode that the modality of the visible is "ineluctable." You can't escape the visible form of the world no matter how hard you try. Thus spake Aristotle. Stephen is wrestling with Proteus, struggling to find answers. Amid

(Continued on bottom of next page)

God becomes man . . . featherbed mountain: the protean, ever-changing, transformation of matter. "Featherbed mountain": a mountain south of Dublin. See, too, Hamlet tracing the movement of Alexander the Great's noble dust (*Hamlet*, Act V, scene 1, 207ff).

Seadeath: The death that Tiresias prophesies for Odysseus "a seaborne death, soft as this hand of mist" (The *Odyssey*, 11:134-35). **Old Father Ocean**: Homeric epithet for Proteus. **Prix de Paris**: Grand Prix de Paris, French: "Great Prize of Paris"—the most important event in the French horseracing calendar. In 1904, the prize itself amounted to 250,000 francs. Stephen is, of course, punning on "the prize of Paris," because Paris, by giving the golden apple to Aphrodite, started the Trojan War and ultimately faced Odysseus with the possibility of "sea death." However, another version of the Helen of Troy story, derived from the Greek poet Stesichorus (632-552 BC), may be relevant. In that version only a ghost, or imitation," of Helen went to Troy with Paris, while the real Helen remained faithful to Menelaus and sat out the Trojan War under the protection of the King of Egypt. Thus, Stephen's thought: **Beware of imitations**, which also sounds somewhat like an advertising slogan, followed by: **Just you give it a fair trial**

Old Father continued from previous page)

all the flux of the world, what remains true? Behind the sensory illusions, where is the absolute reality? He searches for Boehmian mystical signatures, Berkeleyan ideal signs, Blakean primal faculties, the Christian divine substance, the Edenic paradise, the Aristotelian "form of forms," the "word known to all men" that might be love. Stephen's dreams portend—what? How foolish and grandiose he'd been to harbor such egotistical delusions and false hopes? Will anyone ever love him? Know him? And when all is thought, said, and done, will he accomplish the artistic work that he believes he is capable of? Homeless and usurped, will he have to exile himself from the omphalos of Dublin, the city that both nurtured and frustrated his creative gifts?

Menelaus rides Proteus and is given answers. Stephen is left without any certainty about his future. But in the process of his conscious and unconscious struggle, he works through the stifling family connections from which he must eventually free himself, just as he must throw off his continuing attachment to Catholic religion and the alienation he often feels from others. What connects the fluctuating sensations, memories, and images of this episode is the profound passion of his spiritual search. For the rest of the book, we will catch glimpses of Stephen seen through the eyes and actions of Leopold Bloom as they cross paths throughout the day.

In the end, Stephen will walk off into the early hours of the day he is to meet his Nora Barnacle and fulfill his destined self-exile to write the book we are talking about now. This is the last chance we will get to be inside Stephen's consciousness, but through Joyce's consciousness, and the consciousness of the wandering Jew Leopold Bloom, a mood of hopefulness infuses this episode. It is the hope of someone who, despite all the difficulties that lie ahead, can bravely and comically accept the world as it is. In a way, all protagonists of this novel merge in a grand affirmation to life: Yes and a Yes and a Yes.

"Helen of Troy," Dante Gabriel Rossetti, 1799. Public domain, via Wikimedia Commons.

Come. **I thirst**. Clouding over. No black clouds anywhere, are there? Thunderstorm. **Allbright he falls**, proud lightning of the intellect, *Lucifer, dico, qui nescit occasum*. No. **My cockle hat and staff and his my sandal shoon**. Where? **To evening lands**. Evening will find itself.

He took the hilt of his ashplant, lunging with it softly, dallying still. Yes, evening will find itself in me, without me. All days make their end. By the way next when is it **Tuesday will be the longest day**. **Of all the glad new year, mother**, the rum tum tiddledy tum. **Lawn Tennyson**, gentleman poet. **Già**. For the **old hag with the yellow teeth**. And **Monsieur Drumont**, gentleman journalist. *Già*. **My teeth are very bad**. Why, I wonder. Feel. That one is going too. Shells. Ought I go to a dentist, I wonder, with that money? That one. This. Toothless Kinch, **the superman**. Why is that, I wonder, or **does it mean something perhaps?**

Alfred, Lord Tennyson

I cannot rest from travel; I will drink
life to the lees: Greatly, have I suffered,
Always roaming with a hungry heart.
How dull it is to pause, to make an end,
To rust unburnished, not to shine in use!
As though to breathe were life,
But every hour is saved from that eternal
    silence,
something more, a bringer of new things.
This is my son, mine own Telemachus,
When I am gone. He works his work, I mine.
Death closes all; but something ere the end,
Some work of noble note, may yet be done,

'Tis not too late to seek a newer world.
Though much is taken, much abides; and
    though
We are not now that strength which in old
    days
Moved earth and heaven; that which we are,
    we are;
One equal temper of heroic hearts,
Made weak by time and fate, but strong in will
To strive, to seek, to find, and not to yield.
        —From "Ulysses,"
Alfred, Lord Tennyson, 1883
(edited from last 40 lines)

I thirst: Jesus says this on the cross "that the scripture might be fulfilled" (John 19:28). Thus, "thunderstorm" is suggested by the cataclysm after the Crucifixion; and the thunderstorm in turn suggests the fall of Satan. **Allbright he falls . . . occasum**: Lucifer means "light bringing" in Latin; in pride of intellect he refused to serve God and so fell; the phrase in Latin: "The morning star, I say, that [or who] knows no setting." See *Portrait of the Artist*, chapter 3, p 117. *Lucifer, dico, qui nescit occasum*: Latin: "The morning star, I say, who knows no setting." A chant from the Catholic service "acclaiming the light of the risen Christ." While sometimes the morning star refers to Christ, in Isaiah 14:12, it refers to Satan: "How art thou fallen from heaven, O Lucifer, son of the morning."

My cockle hat . . . his my sandal shoon: Ophelia's song in *Hamlet*, IV, scene 5, lines 23 and following:

How should I your true love know from another one?
By his cockle hat and staff, and his sandal shoon.
He is dead and gone; At his head a grass-green turf,
At his heels a stone.

To evening lands: from Shelly's *Helas* (see page); To a sunnier strand, / And follow Love's folding star / To the Evening land!

Tuesday will be the longest day: The novel takes place on June 16, 1904, a Thursday. Tuesday will be June 22, marking the summer solstice (Latin: *solstitium*, "sun-stopping"), the longest day of the year.

Of all the glad new year, Mother: Alfred, Lord Tennyson's (1809-92) "The May Queen" (1833). First verse: "You must wake and call me early, call me early mother dear; / Tomorrow'll be the happiest time of all the glad New Year." **Lawn Tennyson**: Lawn tennis was a genteel version of the modern game—in contrast to court tennis, which was then regarded as a rigorous, demanding, and masculine game. Stephen is belittling the genteel gentleman poet, Tenneyson, who was the official "great poet" of the Victorian age, succeeding Wordsworth as Poet Laureate. Critical reaction to the disproportion of elaborate prosody to often rather flimsy subject matter caused his reputation to rapidly decline in his last years, and his stature as an important poet has only been reestablished in recent times. His poem "Ulysses" still rings true, and Robert Kennedy quoted the last two lines the night he was shot and killed. *Già*: Italian:

For the old hag with the yellow teeth: see note on 88.

Monsieur Drumont: see note on 89.

My teeth are very bad. . . . does it mean something perhaps?: Teeth are the "primigenial weapons of attack;" thus their loss or decay is symbolic of "fear of castration or of complete failure in life, or inhibition" (quoted from a *Dictionary of Symbols*, pg 332). **the superman**: after Nietzsche's *Thus Spoke Zarathustra* (1883). In Episode 1, Buck Mulligan criticizes Stephen: "You could have knelt down, damn it, Kinch, when your mother asked you. I'm hyperborean as much as you, but to think of your mother begging you and you refused. There is something sinister in you." In Greek legend, the *hyperborean* were a mythical people who dwelt beyond the north wind in a perpetual spring without sorrow or old age. The German philosopher Friedrich Nietzsche (1844-1900) refers to the *hyperborean* in his book *The Will to Dominate* (1896) to describe the *Ubermensch*, the superman, who is "above the crowd," not enslaved by conformity to the dictates of Christian morality, whereas the moral man living for others is a weakling, a degenerate.

My handkerchief. He threw it. I remember. Did I not take it up?

His hand groped vainly in his pockets. No, I didn't. Better buy one.

He laid the dry snot picked from his nostril on a ledge of rock, carefully. For the rest let look who will.

Behind. Perhaps there is someone.

He turned his face over a shoulder, **rere regardant**. Moving through the air **high spars of a threemaster,** her sails brailed up on the crosstrees, homing, upstream, silently moving, a silent ship.

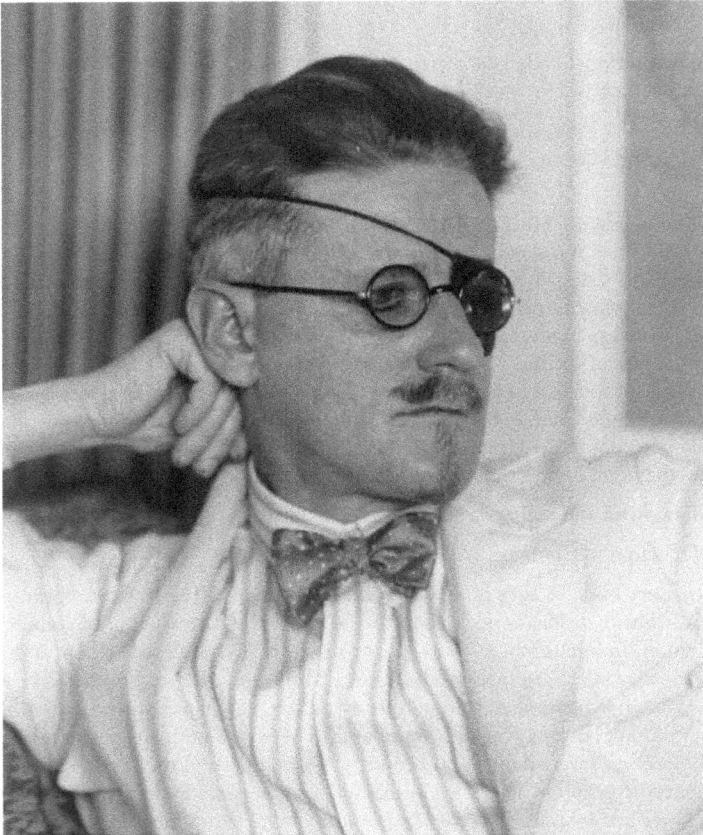

This intimate portrait of Irish writer James Joyce is considered one of the defining images of the author. American photographer Bernice Abbott photographed Joyce on two occasions, the first in 1926 at his home in Paris, the second in 1928 at her studio. Abbott was a former assistant to Man Ray, employing softly diffused lighting to suggest a complex, introverted character. Since the 1910s, Joyce had suffered from eye problems. He had, in all, eleven operations on his eyes and at the time of this photograph was blind in his left eye.

My handkerchief. He threw it: In Episode 1, Buck Mulligan "frowns at the lather on his razor-blade, then reaches into Stephen's coat pocket. "Lend us a loan of your noserag to wipe my razor." After wiping his blade, he intones: "The bard's noserag. A new art colour for our Irish poets: snot-green." Then surveying the sea, he says: "The snotgreen sea. The scrotumtightening sea."

rere regardant: In the language of heraldry: "with the head turned, looking back over the shoulder."

high spars of a three-master: The schooner *Rosevean* announced in "Shipping New," *Freemman's Journal*, 16 June 1904, as "from Bridgewater with bricks;" the three "crosstrees" recall Calvary Hill, where Jesus was crucified with two thieves on either side of him. The sight of the sailing ship is an image of homecoming, just as the *Odyssey* is a tale of the return of a seafarer. At this point in *Ulysses*, Stephen is homeless, and Joyce—self-exiled all his life, living in Trieste, Rome, and Paris—often changed lodgings every few months, and well knew what it was to be homeless.

Photo of the C.A. Thayer, at Gray's Harbor, Oregon, 1903 by unknown author. http://www. nps.gov/archive/safr/local/thhistph.html, Public Domain, https://commons.wikimedia. org/w/index.php?curid=1883059

James Joyce, University College, Dublin, graduation picture, ca. 1902,

Ezra Pound, passport photo, ca. 1903. Source: Yale University Library.

James Joyce photographed in Switzerlamd, 1918. by Conrad Ruf

Ezra Pound photographed in 1913 by Alvin Langdon Coburn.

*James Joyce in his apartment in Rue Edmond-Valentin, Paris, 1939, the year of publication of his final novel, **Finnegans Wake**, two years before his death.*

Ezra Pound, 1963. Photo by Walter Mori (Mondadori Publishers)

Ezra Pound & James Joyce

1914 proved a crucial year for Joyce. With Ezra Pound's assistance, Joyce's first novel, *A Portrait of the Artist as a Young Man*, began to appear in serial form in Harriet Weaver's *Egoist* magazine in London. His collection of short stories, *Dubliners*, on which he had been working since 1904, was finally published, and he also wrote his only play, *Exiles*. Having cleared his desk, Joyce could then start in earnest on the novel he had been thinking about since 1907: *Ulysses*.

In 1913, Joyce received a query from Ezra Pound, who was searching for promising new writers. It wasn't unusual for young writers to network with other young writers, encouraging each other and often promoting others' work. But Ezra Pound was more like a fight promoter when it came to fellow writers. While he ranks among the finest poets of his generation, his greatest trait may have been his eye for talent in others. In addition to advancing the prospects of James Joyce, he also served as mentor and advocate for T.S. Eliot. (Joyce, for his part, later grumbled that Eliot gained renown by borrowing from his *Ulysses*.) Pound also offered encouragement and support to Ernest Hemingway—whom he also introduced to Joyce, Robert Frost, and many other writers and artists. "Ezra was the most generous writer I have ever known," Hemingway later remarked. "He helped poets, painters, sculptors and prose writers that he believed in and he would help anyone whether he believed in them or not if they were in trouble." By Hemingway's estimate, Pound devoted only around one-fifth of his time on his own writing, focusing the rest of his energy on advancing the careers of others. He probably would never have heard of James Joyce had not poet William Butler Yeats mentioned the Irish expat in response to Pound's pointed questioning about possible poets to include in an anthology he was planning.

At the time, Pound held the enviable role of Yeats protégé, serving as the older poet's secretary, house tenant and informal adviser. When Pound mentioned his desire to find new contemporary writers, Yeats remembered the brash newcomer from the latter's time in Ireland, although he may have preferred to forget his dealings with him. One night, wanting to meet the great Irish poet, Joyce sat in front of Yeats' home for hours, waiting for him to come home. Around midnight, tired from a long day, Yeats encountered the young man sitting on his doorstep, and generously invited him in. They talked for several hours. As Joyce got up to leave, the all-but-unknown writer allegedly told the celebrated Irish poet: "You are too old for me to help you." Yeats was taken aback by the younger man's crass audacity, but was nevertheless impressed by Joyce's talent and obvious genius, which made an even deeper impression on him. He remembered something George Russell had told him years before when Russell was describing the impetuous youth. He suggested Yeats meet Mr. Joyce, and in a memorable phrase, added: "I have suffered from him and I would like you to suffer, too."

Pound was twenty years younger than Yeats, and a member of Joyce's generation. On the basis of the older man's recommendation, Pound reached out to his struggling contemporary. In his search for new talent for his anthology, Pound sent the Irish author, who was living in Trieste, a query letter. "Dear Sir," it began, "Mr. Yeats has been speaking to me of your writing." Ezra Pound offered to make useful connections for Joyce, and find places where he could publish his writings. "This is the first time I have written to any one outside of my own circle of acquaintance (save in the case of French authors)," Pound admitted, but he was quick to add: "I don't in the least know that I can be of any use to you—or use to me." These two young men were unlikely allies. In that first letter to Joyce, Pound admitted: "I imagine we have a hate or two in common—but that's a very problematical bond on introduction."

Joyce was thirty years old. He had faced rejection after rejection during the previous decade. He had completed his collection of short stories, *Dubliners*, eight years before Pound contacted him—but Joyce still hadn't found a publisher willing to issue the book. Every time he came close to seeing this work in print, new objections and obstacles arose, and even Joyce's offer to make changes and censor controversial passages failed to remove the roadblocks. Joyce had even fewer prospects to publish his novel *A Portrait of the Artist as a Young Man*. In 1911, his frustration had grown so intense, Joyce threw the manuscript into a fire, and only the quick intervention of his sister Eileen, who pulled the pages out of the flames, prevented the loss of the novel. Joyce had made even less headway with *Ulysses*, a work he had been planning since 1906. His constant financial pressures and despair over his inability to publish his fiction sapped his determination to push ahead with the future masterpiece. Financial struggles were overwhelming. Unable to support himself and his family from his writing, he explored other ways of earning a living. He tried his hand at setting up a chain of movie theaters in Ireland, and worked at importing Irish tweed to Italy. He spent six months in Rome working in a bank. His opportunities to write for hire declined, and most of his income came from teaching English at Berlitz schools. Joyce worked tirelessly at this humble job, but still needed to rely on constant financial support from his brother to pay his bills. Then he received the letter from a writer he'd never heard of. What was there to lose?

Pound was to prove of incalculable value to his new friend. In the coming months, he would arrange for the serialization of *A Portrait of the Artist as a Young Man* in a fashionable literary journal. He sent off Joyce's short stories to H.L. Mencken, the influential American journalist and editor. Pound also featured Joyce's poem "I Hear an Army," written a decade earlier and now all but forgotten, in his anthology of Imagist poetry. But Pound's efforts on Joyce's behalf didn't stop there. He spread word of the Irish author's genius to his numerous contacts in the literary world, and started laying the groundwork for the later success of *Ulysses*. In championing his new discovery, Pound brought his work to the attention of Harriet Weaver, later Joyce's chief financial backer, and Sylvia Beach, the Parisian bookseller who would eventually publish *Ulysses*. In the face of every obstacle stifling Joyce's prospects—financial, editorial, legal—his new American friend searched for solutions, and more often than not found them.

In later years, the two drifted apart. Joyce never had much enthusiasm for Pound's poetry (although it's unclear how much of it he actually read). Pound expressed reservations about Joyce's final work *Finnegans Wake*, and after his move to Rapallo, Italy in 1924, maintained only sporadic contact with the author whose work he had once fiercely championed. At that point, Joyce had little need for Pound. Joyce was now the more famous of the two. Pound, for his own part, was descending into new obsessions, with fascism and amateurish economic theories, fixations that led to ruptures with old friends, a lasting taint on his literary reputation, and perhaps even the unhinging of his mental faculties. Today, young poets and writers still wrestle with their two great works: Joyce's *Ulysses* and Pound's *Cantos*, over a hundred poems written over a period of fifty years. They had a lot in common. Pound set in motion a literary revolution, and Joyce changed the course of modern literature.

Good Friday 29 March 1918, 12:07 a.m.
Dear Joyce: As I wrote this a.m. or yesterday, we have got your first installment into print. 30 copies have reached me here. I suppose we'll be suppressed. The Egoist printers wont set up the stuff at all. I dont mind suppression for the first chapter. Its worth it. Section 4. has excellent things in it; but you overdo the matter. Leave the stool to Geo. Robey a British music-hall comedian known for his toilet humor , he has been doing "down where the asparagus grows" for some time. The contrast between Blooms interior poetry and his outward surroundings is excellent, but it will come up without such detailed treatment of the dropping feces. Perhaps an unexpurgated text of you can be printed in a greek or bulgarian translation later. I'm not even sure "urine" is necessary in the opening page. In the thing as it stands you will lose effectiveness. The excrements will prevent people from noticing the quality of things contrasted. At any rate the thing is risk enough without the full details of the morning deposition.If we are suppressed too often we'll be suppressed finally and for all, to the damn'd stoppage of all our stipends. AND I cant have our august editress jailed, NOT at any rate for a passage which I do not think written with utter maestria. Hence these tears.

Text of a letter Pound sent to Joyce with his original grammar intact.

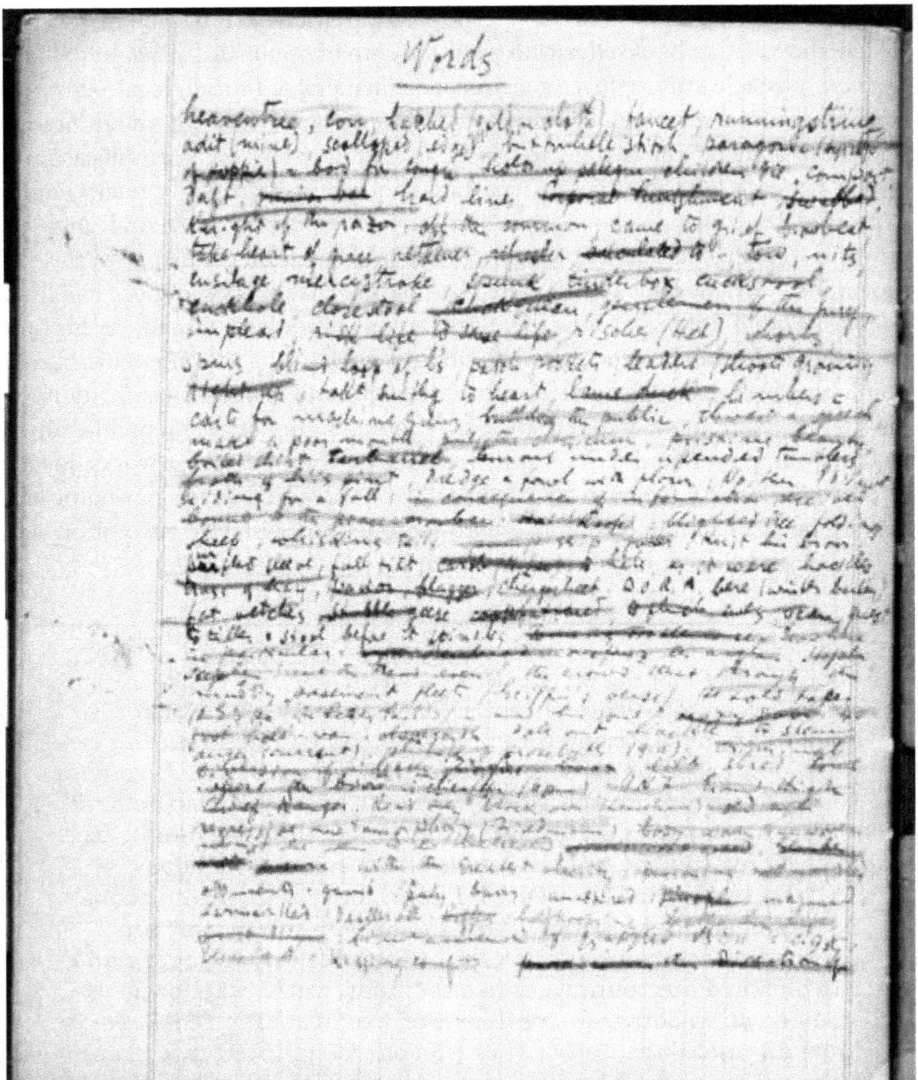

Joyce "wrote lying on his stomach in bed, with a large blue pencil, clad in a white coat," writes ***Brainpickings'*** *Maria Popova. When he was writing* ***Ulysses****, he often scribbled notes on napkins if he was out dining, or on the cuffs of his shirt if he was out drinking. When he came home, he organized all the different notes in different colored envelopes and color coded the envelopes with passages highlighted with crayons. Even today, scholars perusing manuscript pages in Joyce's almost undecipherable handwriting have found it difficult to figure out his colored crayon method. Some edits are not clear on copies made of manuscript pages. Joyce once said about* ***Ulysses****: "I've put in so many enigmas and puzzles that it will keep the professors busy for centuries arguing over what I meant, and that's the only way of insuring one's immortality." Full-blown "Joyceaholic" scholars have devoted their careers to* ***Ulysses****. Those who realized such endeavor was a rabbit hole with no rabbit got out before it became too late. But breaking up is hard to do, and even casual readers of* ***Ulysses*** *have found the book a lifelong passion. And there is no telling where a pub-crawl could end when a "Joyceaholic" meets a "Joyceaholic" coming through the rye. (Image from openculture.com)*

"What Is the Word Known to All Men?"

Anyone who has read James Joyce's *Ulysses* cover to cover is aware that the text is faulty. On the copyright page itself, the publisher asks "the reader's indulgence for typographical errors unavoidable in the exceptional circumstances." Those exceptional circumstances were a rush to publish the novel as a whole in hopes of avoiding a ban on the book, since portions that had already been serialized in American and British literary magazines were deemed obscene, and the editors of those publications faced jail or stiff fines. But errors occurred not just because of a rush to print, but due to the nature of Joyce's text and his own habit of editing even after publication. In the years following its publication, it was difficult for readers to know whether linguistic extravagance was a result of genius or a mistake by the typist or typesetter. Those functionaries should not be derided, for Joyce was obsessively finicky in the presentation of his work on the page, as well the construction of his sentences, half-sentences, puns, and arcane allusions. Grammatical errors intended by Joyce were corrected by well-meaning French typesetters, who thought they were doing Joyce a service. Furthermore, Joyce never stopped revising, even after the first edition was published. Mistakes were inevitable. Soon after Sylvia Beach published the first printing of the first edition on February 2, 1922, Joyce presented her with a list of errata. It was by no means complete. In 1932, his friend Stuart Gilbert, who had become aware of many more errors as he assisted with a translation of the book into French, corrected the text for the *Odyssey* Press edition published in Hamburg. Not all of his changes had Joyce's authorization, however. Finally, in 1936, Joyce proofed the book once more before it was published in London by the Bodley Head. In the years following that edition, there's a long history of conscientious publishers trying to correct misprints, and quite often adding more. A famous instance is the final dot at the end of the penultimate chapter. The dot was assumed to be a flyspeck and was edited out, when in fact it was the obscure answer to the question that ended the episode, *Where?* Joyce gave the printers instructions to enlarge the dot, rather than delete it. That dot has become a litmus test for subsequent editions. If that dot was large, as Joyce intended and as it appears in the first edition, one could trust the editors to be conscientious about the other thousand corrections. A text without the big dot meant other corrections were suspect, or that other errors were overlooked. The 1984 Gabler "Corrected Text" is a case in point. Its missing dot led to one of the biggest feuds in modern literary history.

The most famous correction had to do with the question posed by Stephen Dedalus as he wanders the mud-flats of Sandymount Strand: "What is the word known to all men?", a question he asks again later in the book, where he says, "Tell me Mother, what is the word known to all men?" Did or did he not provide the reader with the answer to that question? In one manuscript of *Ulysses*, Joyce provided the answer, but in subsequent manuscripts and serialized chapters of the novel, and all subsequent editions of the novel, Joyce removed that answer. This has become the linchpin for anyone seeking to produce a perfect edition of *Ulysses*: to include the answer or not to include the answer. In 1984, the "Corrected Text" of *Ulysses* edited by Hans Gabler was published in which the answer was included, and John Kidd launched an attack on that edition in an effort to discredit its authenticity. In one sense, Kidd succeeded; in another, he failed.

The Perfect Edition of *Ulysses*

In 1988, John Kidd, celebrated in his day as one of the greatest Joyce scholars alive, led a team dedicated to a single goal: producing the perfect edition of *Ulysses*, arguably the most-obsessed-over novel of the 20th century. Today, all over the world, lovers of the novel form clubs and stage readings on June 16th, the day on which the action of the novel takes place. That day is now known as "Bloomsday," after the novel's protagonist, Leopold Bloom. The book's action takes place over a 24 hour period and it takes 24 hours to read the book aloud. While there are narrative passages describing particular events of the day, much of the book consists of the observations and fractured bits of memory kicking around in the head of a single schlub named Leopold Bloom as he wanders about Dublin, taking care of business, buying lemon soap and hand lotion for his wife, eating lunch, attending a lecture on Shakespeare, going to a funeral, walking on the beach, stopping by a pub, visiting a friend in the hospital, spending part of the evening in a brothel, and returning home several hours past midnight. Imagine saying to a publisher: "I have a great idea for a novel," then telling him or her this "plot." Who could imagine such a book would be of interest to anyone? Or as Stephen muses in Episode 3, "Who ever anywhere will read these written words?" But Joyce included the interior monologue of the schlub's wife, Molly Bloom, which has proven to be the most famous section of the novel, sometimes performed as a theatrical monologue (I saw Fionnula Flannagan perform it at the Huntington Hartford Theater in the early seventies and it was one of the most memorable nights I've spent in the theatre).

Joyce also devotes three chapters to his alter-ago, Stephen Dedalus, a young writer who has written a series of "epiphanies," some poems, and a couple of polemical essays. Dedalus was the protagonist of Joyce's previous novel, *A Portrait of the Artist as a Young Man*, which ends with Stephen leaving Ireland for Paris to seek his fortune as a writer, invoking his namesake, Daedalus, master craftsman and artist, creator of the labyrinth and father of Icarus:

> Away! Away!
> The spell of arms and voices: the white arms of roads, their promise of close embraces and the black arms of tall ships that stand against the moon, their tale of distant nations. They are

held out to say: We are alone—come. And the voices say with them: We are your kinsmen. And the air is thick with their company as they call to me, their kinsman, making ready to go, shaking the wings of their exultant and terrible youth.

Mother is putting my new secondhand clothes in order. She prays now, she says, that I may learn in my own life and away from home and friends what the heart is and what it feels. Amen. So be it. Welcome, O life! I go to encounter for the millionth time the reality of experience and to forge in the smithy of my soul the uncreated conscience of my race.

Old father, old artificer, stand me now and ever in good stead.

Ulysses begins with Dedalus having just returned from Paris after receiving a telegram from his father that his mother was dying. In the third episode of *Ulysses*, "Proteus," Stephen finds his way to Sandymount Strand and mopes around for awhile, wandering aimlessly on the Strand's mud-flats. In this episode he thinks about his family, his life as a student in Paris, and his mother's death. He also tussles with various philosophical concepts, including the problem of the world's changing face in relation to the reality behind it. This is, perhaps, the densest episode in the novel, a stream of consciousness *tour-de-force*, in which the narrative style changes focus from one flashback to the next. Almost every sentence or phrase alludes to philosophical ideas, historical events, obscure references and foreign phrases. It is no wonder the chapter has earned a reputation as one of the book's most difficult. Joyce himself said: "I've put in so many enigmas and puzzles that the book will keep the professors busy for centuries arguing over what I meant." Part of the experience for those who have confronted "the book" (Joyce never called it a novel, only "the book") is the pleasure of assembling those bits and pieces to produce a small section of the vast canvas Joyce created. Those bits and pieces of consciousness, description, and prose add up to a style that mimics almost every style and genre of writing from Homer to the present: For example, in Episode 12, "The Cyclops," the narrative is punctuated by 33 commentaries, or "interpolations," in vastly different styles, with each style an inflated caricature of the legal, the poetic epic, the scientific, the journalistic, and so on, where the tragic and comic mood exist side by side, where the poetic and vulgar are intertwined. As a reader, when those moments of "getting it" suddenly happen, the reward is unlike the experience of reading any other book. As a matter of fact, one doesn't "read" *Ulysses*. One "encounters" it, one "confronts" it. And when the dust of all the allusions and linguistic showmanship have settled, one is left with the indelible story of that Irish schlub, his lusty wife, and the young writer who encounters them.

A Problematic Text

Joyce wrote *Ulysses* over a period of seven years, amid the First World War and personal chaos. Not long after the book was published in 1922, Joyce was besieged with poverty and illness. The walking stick "that he used for swagger as a young bachelor," Kevin Birmingham writes in *The Most Dangerous Book*, "became a blind man's cane in Paris." If the stereotype of a writer in exile (usually Paris) working in cold-water poverty on his masterpiece is branded somewhere in your mind, that cliché owes something to the lived reality of James Joyce. Unlike F. Scott Fitzgerald, for instance, who carefully plotted his novels, obsessively outlining almost every scene as if it were a screenplay, Joyce approached his creative work in a scattershot manner, scribbling in notebooks and on handy scraps of paper. When he was out with friends, they saw him write on the cuffs of his shirts, either before or after having drunk too much and doing his famous "spider dance." He sketched dialogue or description in notebooks and stuffed random notes in color-coded envelopes. When parts of the novel were published in magazines, he revised them even further. In 1922, when *Ulysses* first appeared, all that partially illegible handwriting was botched into print by French typesetters, most of whom spoke no English, and those who could were mystified by his syntax, diction, the inclusion of foreign languages, literary allusions and unorthodox typographical instructions. Joyce himself was perhaps the only person qualified to proofread the manuscripts, but he seemed more eager to add text than to edit his proofs, even in the late stages of editing. The original edition was plagued with errors, misspellings, misplaced commas, and, in a few instances, missing pages. (I discovered decades later that the copy I had used in college was missing about thirty pages in Episode 8, where Stephen lectures on *Hamlet* at the National Library—thanks to Joyce's convoluted syntax and jumps in logical coherence, I hadn't even noticed it.) In all, that first edition contained several thousand errors.

Even before its formal publication as a book on his birthday, February 2, 1922, the text of *Ulysses* was problematic. Five sections had appeared in 1919 in *The Egoist*, a London magazine edited by Harriet Shaw Weaver, who ran into problems with her printers and a revolt from some subscribers. Between 1918 and 1920, parts of the book appeared in serial form in *The Little Review*, an avant-garde American magazine edited by Margaret Anderson and Jane Heap. By February 1921, the magazine had been found guilty of obscenity and the editors fined. Harriet Weaver turned the *Egoist* into the Egoist Press to publish the entire book, but soon concluded that no British printer, for fear of libel and obscenity laws, would take it on. In desperation, Joyce turned to Sylvia Beach, the American owner of Shakespeare and Company, the expatriate bookstore in Paris, and asked her to publish the book in France. She agreed. The printer was Maurice Darantière from Dijon. *Ulysses* would be sold by subscription only;

copies would have to be smuggled into the United States and Britain. Joyce was still in the process of writing the final half-dozen episodes while the earlier ones, which had been serialized, were being typeset. Each episode became more complex than the last, necessitating his going back over the earlier episodes and adding more text to conform to what the book was becoming. If you compare the first six episodes that appeared in serialized form with those same six episodes as they appeared in the first edition, it becomes apparent that Joyce often added at least one-third more text. Throughout this period of gestation, Joyce had sold or given draft versions of earlier sections of *Ulysses* to well-wishers. It had been his habit to procure three copies of each of his chapters from typists (one typist's husband caught a glimpse of a page and burned both what she had typed and the manuscript chapter as well). Joyce then made revisions on two of the typed copies (often scribbling additions in the margins and cutting whole paragraphs)—one to be sent to *The Egoist*, the other to be sent to *The Little Review*. To the printer, Darantière, he could supply only the third copy, which he revised and corrected as best he could, working from memory, whatever copies of published chapters he could find, and, in all likelihood, further artistic inspiration. By the time he received galley-proofs from Darantière, the thin line between editorial correcting proofing, and creative rewriting, had all but disappeared: invention was piled upon correction, addition upon amendment, with the result that *Ulysses* expanded massively in proof. This was particularly true of the later episodes which were being rewritten at the same time. Joyce was in a rush to finish those final chapters and get the whole book into print, believing that there was a better chance the book would not be banned for obscenity if the offending passages were measured against the whole of the book. If he had not been afraid of the book being banned, the fear of copies being destroyed by the authorities—Joyce may have taken even longer to finish the novel. In any case, and right on time, the first two copies, hot off the press, were hand-delivered to Sylvia Beach and Joyce by the conductor of the train from Dijon at 7 A.M. on the morning of February 2, 1922, Joyce's fortieth birthday. Soon, Beach, Joyce, and all who worked at the bookstore were busy dispatching copies to subscribers all over the world. Officially, the book was immediately banned in the United States. A notorious pornographer capitalized on this opportunity by rushing a pirated and even more corrupt edition into print. The first Shakespeare and Company edition consisted of 1,000 copies, 100 of which were printed on Dutch handmade paper numbered from 1 to 100 and signed by the author; 150 copies were printed on Vergé D'Arches numbered from 101 to 250; and 750 copies were printed on handmade paper numbered from 251 to 1,000. A note from the publisher asked "the reader's indulgence for typographical errors unavoidable in the exceptional circumstances." Actual copies of that first edition are now among the rarest and most valuable volumes in the modernist rare books trade for first editions published in the 20th Century. (Most valuable first editions of all time include the Gutenberg Bible [$5 million], Shakespeare's *First Folio,* [$6 million], and John James Audubon's *Birds of America* [$11 million], depending on condition and other factors.)

Editions of *Ulysses* Published Since 1922

A second edition of two thousand copies was brought out in October by the Egoist Press in London, with Darantière again serving as printer. 500 of those copies were detained by the New York Post Office Authority and several hundred confiscated in Britain. In January 1924, Shakespeare and Company published an unlimited edition, which was reset in 1926. That same month, a manuscript of *Ulysses* (comprising the first twelve chapters) which Joyce had sold a few episodes at a time to the New York lawyer John Quinn, was auctioned to a Dr. A. Rosenbach (referred to as the *Rosenbach Manuscript*). In 1932, an Odyssey Press edition appeared in Hamburg. Joyce's friend and confidant, Stuart Gilbert, shepherded it through the printing with more edits, corrections, additions, and a like amount of new errors and typos. Three years later Joyce made more suggestions to Gilbert, which were incorporated in a Limited Edition Club version with illustrations by Henri Matisse. Finally, in 1933, a federal judge in the United States ruled in favor of publishing the novel, and Random House accidentally relied on that wildly corrupt pirated text to produce the official *Ulysses* in America. Two years later, in 1936, the Bodley Head brought out its famous thousand-copy British edition, proofed by Joyce (bad eyesight and all) the previous summer, with 100 copies signed by him. These two editions—the Random House and Bodley Head became the standard versions. The Random House edition (based on that corrupt text) would go on to occupy American bookshelves for several decades before they issued a "revised" edition in 1961, though that one too contained thousands of errors, most of them from the original 1922 edition. Bodley Head brought out new editions with some corrections (and more errors) in 1941, 1947, and 1949 (Joyce died in 1941). In 1968, Penguin Books in London brought out an unlimited edition, reset, with many errors corrected and, as usual, new ones cropping up. In 1991, to coincide with the fiftieth anniversary of Joyce's death, Penguin brought out another reset edition based on the Random House/Bodley Head text that had first appeared in 1961. Numerous other editions have appeared, all fixing hundreds of errors only to create hundreds more. For every error corrected, two more were made, either through careless typesetting, confusion regarding the word Joyce originally intended, or basic stupidity. *Ulysses* became an odyssey of errors. The idea of a "definitive" text remained a chimera.

The Attempt to Produce a Definitive Text

For years, rumors persisted that some textual fanatic was about to take on the task of cleaning it all up, but no scholar realized that dream. John Dalton was said to be working on one, but he became overwhelmed by the project and died in 1981 without producing the hoped for edition. Then, in the late 1970s, the Munich scholar Hans Walter Gabler, trained in the rigorous textual editing school of the University of Virginia, received a six-figure grant from the German government to undertake the project of producing a "corrected" text. He assembled a team of scholars and research assistants, and fine-tooth combed through manuscripts and copy-sheets, one word at a time, using a new textual theory that almost no one understood. Computers were used to collate the many manuscript pages, typescripts, proofs, and editions. His rationale for this procedure was fairly complex. Typist and typesetter had tended to conventionalize Joyce's mannered punctuation and spelling, and Joyce, on the lookout for large issues, did not always notice details of this kind. What Gabler aimed at was an ideal text, such as Joyce would have constructed in ideal conditions. Mr. Gabler and his team of scholars labored for seven years. Many of the corrections were rather minor, but others were substantive. For instance, in the previous editions, Bloom, as he looks in the window of a tea merchant, feels the heat:

> So warm. His right hand once more slowly went over again:
> choice blend, made of the finest Ceylon brands.

The fact that it makes no sense doesn't necessarily interfere with the stream-of-consciousness flow, but Gabler found this passage phrased more clearly in a previous manuscript as

> So warm. His right hand once more slowly went over his brow
> and hair. Then he put on his hat again, relieved: and read again:
> choice blend, made of the finest Ceylon brands.

As Stephen walks along Sandymount strand, in the original edition,

> Unwholesome sandflats waited to suck his treading soles,
> breathing upward sewage breath.

The new edition shows that Joyce intended a more elaborate fusion of water and fire:

> Unwholesome sandflats waited to suck his treading soles,
> breathing upward sewage breath, a pocket of seaweed smoul-
> dered in seafire under a midden of man's ashes.

The problem with revised editions was they often fixed hundreds of errors while creating hundreds of new errors, whether mere typos or inadvertent corrections of misspelled words that Joyce had purposely misspelled, for one reason or another. For instance, the famous telegram from Simon Dedalus to Stephen did not read when delivered to him in Paris, "Mother dying come home father," but "Nother dying come home father." Hence it was, as Stephen recalls in the "Proteus" episode, a "curiosity to show." The typesetters could not believe their eyes in this instance, nor in another when Bella Cohen's favorite customer asks, "Have you forgotten me?" and is answered, "Nes. Yo." They changed it to "Yes. No." But the Gabler text purported to be an ideal text, the text Joyce would have wanted. It was finally published in a critical and synoptic three-volume scholarly edition in 1984 and came out in paperback in 1986 as the "Corrected Text" by Vintage books, a division of Random House. Gabler had the full backing of the Joyce Estate, which encouraged Mr. Gabler to include "a significant amount of fresh material." Gabler made some startling claims for his work. He argued that he was able to offer about five-thousand improvements on the 1922 and 1961 editions, both of which were regarded by textualists at that time as the appropriate bases for further scholarly refinement. Gabler's method was considered revolutionary: he redefined as a "continuous manuscript text" all of the drafts, notebooks, manuscripts, typescripts, corrected and uncorrected proofs and various editions overseen by Joyce, who, Gabler claimed, was to be imagined as a writer of a "continuous copy." With the help of a sophisticated computer, an ideal *Ulysses* might be reconstructed from this evolving archive. Where previous editors were baffled by the plethora of materials left over from the composition process and multiplicity of editions, his team saw the proliferation of versions as a godsend, enabling a definitive reconstruction. But given its disorderly gestation, there were many who warned that there could never be a definitive *Ulysses*. Most of the criticism Gabler received since this corrected text was published focused on the "fresh material" that Joyce may or may not have intended to be included in the final edition. So why this extensive search for "fresh material" of dubious authenticity? One theory has it that Random House and the Joyce Estate wished to add enough material to allow the establishment of a new 75-year copyright term that would have started on the book's new publication date, leaving the Joyce Estate and Random House rolling in *Ulysses* money well into the next century.

Is a Definitive Edition of *Ulysses* Even Possible?

Initially, the Gabler "Corrected Edition" was met with high praise. The esteemed Joycean Richard Ellmann called it "the ideal text." I'm no Joycean scholar, by any means, but when I read the Gabler version, I was struck by the presentation of the headlines Joyce used in Episode 7, "Aeolus," which takes place in the offices of the *Weekly Freeman and National Press,* the *Freeman's Journal and National Press,* and the *Telegraph,* another Dublin newspaper, all of which were in the same building because the papers were under common ownership.

In both the 1922 first edition and the 1961 Random House revised edition, the headlines were printed in large bold letters, mimicking a newspaper headline. A few years ago, I attended a Bloomsday celebration at the Hammer Museum. A staged reading of that episode featured rear screen projections of those headlines. The Gabler edition put those headlines in all caps, but not in bold type, nor was the font much bigger than the text itself. Being a stickler, myself, for graphic elements in my own poems, this struck me as odd. With all the computers and manuscripts at their disposal, how could they have failed to notice that Joyce cleverly divided that episode into short sections featuring bold newspaper style headlines? I found this annoying, to say the least. But it indicated a careless disregard for authenticity while pursuing a goal to pad the book with enough "fresh material" to extend the copyright, which in Europe was due to expire in 1992, and in America . . . . well, that is still open to legal debate. At the time, *Ulysses* sold an estimated 100,000 copies a year. A renewal of copyright would protect revenues for decades to come, for both the publisher and Stephen Joyce, Joyce's Grandson, who had to legally authorize Gabler's new edition. Upon further research, I discovered that John Kidd, that celebrated Joycean scholar, had already noted that something was amiss.

The Scandal of *Ulysses*

As a graduate student, Kidd had visited Mr. Gabler's Munich offices and was distressed by his elder's methods, which he described as "superficial, based on the crudest facsimiles with the minimum attention to originals." When Gabler's edition came out, Kidd was still a postdoctoral candidate. Nevertheless, he undertook an intense scrutiny of Gabler's changes and research methods, inspired, he said, out of sympathy for Joyce's novel. "It's like my thing with animals," he said. "You see this animal that's hurt—what do you do, just walk by?" A year after the Gabler edition appeared, the literary gunfight at the Society for Textual Scholarship took place. In a paper called "Errors of Execution in the 1984 *Ulysses*," Kidd presented his criticisms. Gabler, as it turned out, had received an advance copy of the paper and showed up with his own guns blazing: a 10-page rebuttal in which he called the criticisms by this academic nobody "unfounded and misconceived." A year later, in a lengthy *New York Review of Books* article called "The Scandal of *Ulysses*," Kidd tore apart Gabler's edition, dismantling it mistake by mistake, accusing Gabler of "shoddy scholarship, puffed out with grandiose claims." In retaliation, a Gablerite circulated an article in which he described Kidd as "drooling away in bewildering gibberish." Some of Kidd's objections seemed inconsequential, but many of them fundamentally affected the novel, and it was those objections that made the case for significant "corrections." Of all the issues Kidd raised, perhaps the most significant was the question posed by Stephen, "What is the word known to all men?" For those who have read the book, the question is posed twice, once in Episode 3, "Proteus," and again in Episode 15, "Circe," to his dead mother. Except for a mention in the *Rosenbach Manuscript* (Episode 9, "Scylla and Charybdis") Joyce never provides an answer to this question. The question itself is so majestic that we find ourselves frustrated by Joyce's refusal to provide an answer, while at the same time delighting in his decision to maintain the mystery. Is it the word "death?" Is it "God?" Is it some obscure Greek term (a Joycean specialty —*synteresis* maybe, which, according to the *Catholic Encyclopedia*, is a term used by the Scholastic theologians to signify "the habitual knowledge of the universal practical principles of moral action," or put simply, the will to act toward the good). Some scholars and non-academic readers have pointed to Episode 12, "Cyclops," where Bloom is harassed in Barney Kiernan's pub by the anti-Semitic nationalist Citizen and his terrifying dog, Garryowen. At one point the Citizen proclaims: "There's a Jew for you! Cute as a shithouse rat." Bloom defends himself:

> —And I belong to a race too, says Bloom, that is hated and persecuted. Also now. This very moment. This very instant. Robbed. Plundered. Insulted. Persecuted. Taking what belongs to us by right. At this very moment, says he, putting up his fist, sold by auction off in Morocco like slaves or cattles.
> —Are you talking about the new Jerusalem? says the Citizen.
> —I'm talking about injustice, says Bloom. . . . But it's no use, says he. Force, hatred, history, all that. That's not life for men and women, insult and hatred. And everybody knows that it's the very opposite of that that is really life.
> —What? says Alf.
> —Love, says Bloom. I mean the opposite of hatred.
> —A new apostle to the gentiles, says the Citizen. Universal love.
> —Well, says John Wyse, isn't that what we're told? Love your neighbors.
> —That chap? says the Citizen. Beggar my neighbor is his motto. Love, Moya! He's a nice pattern of a Romeo and Juliet.
> Love loves to love love. . . . . Everybody loves somebody but God loves everybody.
>
> [this is the nameless narrator of this episode
> quoting St. Augustine's discussion of God's
> love in chapter 3 of his *Confessions*.]

Bloom reminds them that the foundation of Christianity is love. So is "love" the word known to all men? Or is it injustice? If Joyce had provided the answer, it would have limited the amplitude of the mental tremors emanating from such a question. Instead, Joyce got what he wanted: Readers and professors and scholars have argued his question for almost a century. Imagine an editor saying he'd found new parts of *Hamlet*, and the new edition read: "To be or not to be, that is the question," followed by "and the answer is definitely 'be.'" Well, this is what Gabler did. He found a passage in the *Rosenbach Manuscript* where Joyce did reveal the answer, but it disappeared in subsequent drafts of that episode. Gabler decided (upon what evidence, we wonder) that it was nothing more than a typist's error. And so, in a novel famous for its elliptical style, the reader now comes across a passage in Gabler's "corrected" edition containing this sentence: "Love, yes. Word known to all men." Like the reduction of the newspaper headlines into smaller un-bolded caps, this revelation obliterates one of the book's most important "puzzles." Kidd criticized Gabler by saying that "the Corrected Text is marbled with the fat of such pseudo-restorations from shoulder to shank!"

But was Joyce so fastidious that he would argue over the size of a period? He was, and he did. In Molly Bloom's soliloquy, which ends the novel, none of the eight, long, meandering stream-of-consciousness sentences ends in a period—except for the very last sentence, and the one sentence in the middle which ends "as for being a woman as soon as youre old they might as well throw you out in the bottom of the ash pit." Period! Joyce was firm about this (The Penguin paperback edition, reset in 1968 and reissued in 1991 fails to include this period, even though they claim it was based on the Random House / Bodley Head edition, which *did* include the period). But Joyce was even firmer about another period, the one that ended the episode that preceded Molly's soliloquy, Episode 17, "Ithaca." He wanted that period to be larger than the usual period. Joyce worried over its size, instructing his French printers to make the first edition's big dot darker and even "more visible." I checked my facsimile copy of the first edition with its "Agean-Blue" cover, and sure enough, the dot at the end of the penultimate episode is quite visible, more a square than a dot:

■ In the Random House/Modern Library 1934/1961 edition, it's a big round dot: ●. This big typographic "dot" ends a long, hilarious chapter that parodies the kind of crisp, cold tone associated with scientific discourse. The Q. and A. format is precise to the point of exasperation. By the end of the episode, after hundreds of questions—"In what directions did listener and narrator lie?" "In what posture?"—the pesky interrogator finally asks, "Where?" To which Joyce drops his big fat dot, as if to say: "Just shut up." (The big dot is also missing in the Penguin Edition.) Interpretations of this dot, to say the least, abound, including Anthony Burgess's suggestion that when reading the text aloud, the dot should be pronounced as one big snore. Some think of it as a portal, others that it represents Molly's anus—recalling the answer to a previous question asking what Bloom did next after climbing in bed and lying head to foot and foot to head, next to Molly, his face against her backside: "He kissed the plump mellow yellow smellow melons of her rump, on each plump melonous hemisphere, in their mellow yellow furrow, with obscure prolonged provocative melonsmellonous osculation." In the current Random House edition, it's there, final, huge—an inky one-eighth of an inch in diameter, the head of a twopenny nail stabbed into the book. But for some reason, Gabler's dot is barely larger than the period at the end of this sentence. When asked about it, Gabler huffily said that even though the dot is not a large one, "it is a very black one."

The Fog of Greed

In the Fall 1985 issue of *The Irish Literary Supplement* on "Gaelic in the New *Ulysses*," Kidd argued that Gabler's treatment of Irish-language words and phrases was symptomatic of a pervasive sloppiness. "A comprehensive computer-file" had given way to "a human wish-list," he wrote. His conclusion was emphatic: "By no means should the proposed text be favored over editions already in print." Many of Kidd's other points had been anticipated by the Irish scholar Vivian Mercier in a talk given in Dublin in 1985. An extended debate was called for by many scholars, but Gabler stood his ground—more was at stake than one man's reputation. If the "Corrected Text" was not accepted, Gabler's publisher stood to lose hundreds of thousands of dollars. Finally, at a conference in Monaco, Fritz Stenn argued that there really was no "continuous manuscript text" since the entire work did not exist in Joyce's hand. C. H. Peake argued that in the first three episodes, the final wording in the 1922 text was closer to Joyce's final revisions than was the Gabler edition. Giovanni Cianci found fault with the typography of Episode 7, "Aeolus," featuring those bold newspaper headlines, which Joyce took such pains to make larger and darker. Gabler inexplicably reduced those bold headlines to smaller type and used all caps, which appeared fainter than the bold headlines used in the 1922 edition. Gabler never offered a rationale for such a change. In each of these cases, the 1922 first edition, as well as the Random House / Modern Library 1961 edition seemed preferable to Gabler's. The final blow to the "Corrected Text" was Richard Ellman's withdrawal of his earlier support for the most famous change in the 1984 version, the insertion of the words "Love, yes. Word known to all men." Ellman had written the preface to the Gabler edition, noting that "the most significant of the many small changes in Gabler's text has to do with the question that Stephen puts to his mother at the climax of the brothel scene, itself the climax of the novel."

> Stephen is appalled by his mother's ghost, but like Ulysses he seeks information from her. His mother says "You sang that song to me, *Love's bitter mystery.*" Stephen responds "eagerly," as the stage directions says, "Tell me the word, mother, if you know now. The word known to all men." She failed to provide it. This passage has been much interpreted. Gabler has been

able to settle this matter by recovering a passage left out of the scene that takes place in the National Library [in Episode 9, "Scylla and Charybdis"]. Whether Joyce omitted it deliberately or not is still a matter of conjecture and debate. Gabler postulates an eyeskip from one ellipsis to another, leading to the omission of several lines—the longest omission in the book. These lines read in [the Rosenbach] Manuscript

> Do you know what you are talking about? Love, yes. Word known to all men. *Amor vero aliquid alicui bonum vult unde et ea quae concupiscimus . . .*

The Latin conjoins two phrases in Thomas Aquinas's *Summa contra gentiles*. Aquinas is distinguishing between love, which as he says in the first six words, "genuinely wishes another's good," and, in the next five, a selfish desire to secure our own pleasure "on account of which we desire these things," meaning lovelessly and for our own good, not another's.

One can understand Ellman's eagerness to endorse Gabler's decision to include those sentences from the *Rosenbach Manuscript*, since Ellman had always believed that love was the underlying message of the novel. After all, what had Stephen's mother wished for him at the conclusion of *A Portrait of the Artist?* "She prays now that I may learn in my own life and away from home and friends what the heart is and what it feels." Furthermore, in Joyce's play *Exiles* Richard explains love to the skeptical Robert as meaning "to wish someone well." In accepting this view, Stephen Dedalus is following his master Dante, who has Virgil say, in Canto XVII of the *Purgatorio*—that canto in which the meaning of purgatory is set forth and Virgil discourses on love—*Né creator né creatura, mai figliuol, fu sanza amore, o naturale o d'animo; e tu 'l sai.*—"Neither Creator nor creature, my son, was ever without love, whether natural or of the mind, and this you know." But Kidd pointed out some problems with this, and eventually, Ellman realized he could not endorse Gabler decision to include those sentences found only in the *Rosenbach Manuscript*, sentences Joyce had removed in all subsequent manuscripts and editions. For one thing, the quote by Aquinas was a jumbled Latin quotation. The Latin was soon revealed to be a conflation of two fragments by Thomas Aquinas in his *Summa Contra Gentiles*, and this led Ellman to infer that Joyce, recognizing the impenetrability of the quotation, wisely decided to remove it (despite having retained it in the *Rosenbach Manuscript*). Even operating under the notion of a "continuous manuscript," adding both the quote about "love" and the Aquinas quotes made no sense, unless the ultimate objective was to find an excuse to add "fresh text" in order to secure a new copyright. Ellman, who had always argued that love was the central theme of *Ulysses*, nevertheless concluded that the quote with the word "love" should not have been re-inserted into the text. Joyce, he realized, would not have permitted Stephen to proclaim the word (in Episode 9) hundreds of pages before he asks his dead mother to name it (in Episode 15).

Eventually, it became clear that the 1984 "Corrected Text" of *Ulysses* was filled with blunders. Because he worked from facsimiles instead of the original manuscripts, Gabler was often unable to distinguish small errors that would have been clearer had he been able to use the originals, even those with Joyce's often illegible handwriting. It was also difficult to tell which corrections written in the margins were from the printers or the proofreaders. Kidd contended that the new text overrode what Joyce actually wrote on two thousand occasions, listing thirteen categories of such changes, including alterations to spelling, italics, punctuation, names, typographical features, numbers, capitalizations, literary allusions and foreign languages. In the end, scholars backed Kidd. The brash young scholar had outgunned the corporate gunslinger. Gabler's enterprise was tainted by the fog of greed. The Gabler "Corrected Text" was called by Kidd "a different version from what Joyce conceived, authorized, and saw into print." It was not a corrected text at all, but a new one altogether, and not to be relied upon as definitive. Until *Ulysses* was meticulously edited afresh, Kidd said, with scholarly and financial help from a foundation, the Bodley Head/Random House edition, "the book roughly as Joyce last saw it, is the best we have." What was Random House to do? They reissued the 1961 edition, however corrupt it might be, acknowledging that the Gabler text was not an improvement after all. But they kept both editions in print. The 1961 "Revised Edition" now slightly outsells Gabler's "Corrected Text." For his part, Joyce's notoriously prickly grandson, Stephen Joyce, who heads the Joyce Estate, called for a "plague" upon all Joyce scholars.

Which Edition Should You Read?

While the original first edition is available only to collectors able to pay millions, you can get through Amazon a facsimile reproduction of the original 1922 text, though one must remember it was riddled with close to two thousand errors, but as errors go, it's no worse than the thousand or so in any of the other editions. So there's something to be said for reading the text as it first appeared on Joyce's fortieth birthday, February 2, 1922, or as Joyce liked to think of it—2-2-22. But for readability and durability, I prefer the 1961 "Revised" Random House edition, in their Modern Library binding, easy to read, easy to make notes in the margins, and more durable than a paperback, though it too has several thousand errors. That edition was revised again in 1992 with page numbers from the 1934 first American edition indicated in parentheses in the margins for easy comparison. In 1998, the Oxford University Press issued a reproduction of the 1922 first edition, copy no. 785 in the Bodleian Library, reisssued in 2008 as an Oxford World Classic, with explanatory notes in the back by Jeri Johnson. The only drawback is the small type which is hard to read, and it's bulky, as far as paperbacks go. There's also a Penguin edition that uses the Random House/Bodley Head text, but it's not a facsimile. The type is large but looks cramped and it has its own set of errors, including the lack of those bold headlines in Episode 7 and the absence of our beloved big fat dot at the end of Episode 17. Then there's the Gabler "Corrected Text." Should you become infected with the Joycean bug, you will probably end up obsessively reading all four of those editions out of curiosity, as I did. My recommendation: get both the Random House Modern Library edition for readability and durability, but keep the Oxford World Classic next to it so you can refer to the notes at the end, as well as Johnson's summary of each episode.

Will There Ever Be a Definitive Version of *Ulysses*?

What about that definitive edition? Kidd was supposed to be working on it. Boston University made him director of the James Joyce Research Center where he worked in a suite of offices dedicated to the study of *Ulysses*. His goal: to produce a perfect edition of the text. Word is that he produced a digital edition, one that used embedded hyperlinks to make the novel's vast thicket of references and allusions, patterns and connections all available at a click. Then, Kidd simply vanished. One of his colleagues on the faculty at Boston University, Faulkner scholar John Matthews, wrote, "I'd heard that he died, and I suspect that actually is true. . . .Kidd was a public eccentric in town—the whole 'talking to the squirrels' deal. A sad ending." James Winn, a Dryden scholar, said he'd heard rumors of his death "but nothing substantive." Jack Hitt, in an article for the *New York Times Magazine*, "The Strange Case of the Missing Joyce Scholar," came upon a Romanian scholar, Mircea Mihaies, who had written a history of *Ulysses*. He confirmed the rumor, saying in an interview that John Kidd "died under sordid circumstances in 2010, buried in debt, detested, insulted, alone, abandoned by everyone, communicating only with pigeons on a Boston campus."

The Missing Scholar Found

Years earlier, when Kidd was still at Boston University, Jack Hitt had contacted him about working on an article together, but they never met and nothing came of it. In 2017, Hitt heard about Kidd's strange demise, but when he looked into it, he could find no obituary. Sniffing a story, he contacted all the homeless shelters in Brookline. Then he wrote to all of Kidd's colleagues. One professor wrote back that he'd heard that Kidd had moved to South America. After much sleuthing, he was given an old email address for Kidd, sent a note to him, and a few days later, got this back from Kidd: "I remember you very well . . . . When do you plan to be in Rio?" Hitt jumped on a plane and waiting for him at the airport was John Kidd, no longer the young firebrand with short blond hair. Kidd was 65, well over 6 feet tall with long snowy white hair, wearing a loose-fitting Hawaiian shirt, flip-flops and shorts. They drove to his apartment, a unit in a high rise with a gorgeous view of Rio. The walls were covered with books. There were lots of bureaus and built-in dressers, every drawer packed top to bottom, side to side, with even more books. Miffed about the *Boston Globe* article that claimed he was "broke," he produced a notarized letter from Fleet Bank stating: "six months avg balance in this checking account has been $15,618." As far as Boston University was concerned, Kidd had simply quit. He lingered on campus for a while, haunting Marsh Plaza, then set off for Beijing. Once there, he read China's great epic novel, *Dream of the Red Chamber*, and became a "redologist," an actual term for those who submerge themselves in the study of this one book. Later, he moved to Brazil, became fluent in Portuguese, then became obsessed with *The Slave of Isaura*, Brazil's version of *Uncle Tom's Cabin*, a popular work that in its early days had helped to end slavery. He worked nearby at the Brazilian Academy of Letters translating *The Slave of Isaura*—which is nearly twice as thick as Joyce's *Ulysses*—into English. His translation will be titled *Isaura Unbound*.

As far as the perfect *Ulysses* is concerned, Kidd admitted that he had assembled a draft of an edition with a complete introduction. One of Kidd's editors at Norton, Julie Reidhead, confirmed the draft existed but said that one delay after another—"an infinite loop of revision"—ran into the legal wall of new copyright extensions, and so Norton "stopped the project." One Joyce scholar remembers reading the introduction but no longer has a copy, and Kidd doesn't have one either. Arion Press issued a new edition of *Ulysses* that included some of the preliminary Kidd edits. The book was luxurious, with prints by Robert Motherwell, and only 175 of them were printed. If you're lucky, you might find a copy being offered on sale for $25,000. Kidd's digital edition is still a dream.

So where do we stand 25 years after the Joyce wars? The Gabler "Corrected Text" thrives because it's a preferred edition by many academics, mainly because it can be cited by line numbers, making it handy for critical articles. Had Kidd been able to publish his own edition, it would surely have supplanted the Gabler text. But in the years since, even those academics and scholars who accepted Kidd's criticisms have now made their peace with the Gabler text. It's been a quiet transition, no big pronouncements, but both the "Corrected Text" and the Random House/Modern Library Edition sell well. So does the Oxford World Classics edition, mainly because it's the original 1922 text (with all those original errors) and because it has a good introduction and annotations by Jeri Johnson. Granted, since the original edition fell out of copyright in the mid-1990s, some editors rushed to publish their own editions, some of which have dots, some of which do not. Some contain the answer to Stephen's question ("love"), some do not. Some reversed a selection of Gabler's changes, some did not. Some editions have gone off the rails, as the Joyce scholar Sam Slote noted: One *Ulysses,* currently available online, has a long, bizarre riff inserted on page 160, announcing that you will now be reading "The Secret Confessions of a Conservative," where the anonymous writer explains that his pro-life, pro-death-penalty positions are so consistent that "if an embryo or fetus commits murder, then he should be aborted." *Ulysses* is so encyclopedic, that one could easily assume that such passages are Joyce's.

Right now, on Amazon alone, there are nearly a dozen slightly different versions of the novel "as James Joyce wrote it." None of them are perfect, but each of them is *Ulysses,* which is why I favor the one easiest to hold and read (the Random House edition) and the one with extensive annotations and notes (the Oxford World Classic Edition). Whichever edition you read, it will be the beginning of a lifelong friendship, a voyage, not unlike Odysseus's, during which you will encounter beautiful prose, arcane allusions, manifold associations, emotional scenes, shocking images, and heartfelt yearnings for—perhaps this is the word known to all men—home.

Sylvia Beach and James Joyce

www.ingramcontent.com/pod-product-compliance
Lightning Source LLC
Chambersburg PA
CBHW071756090426
42737CB00012B/1844